The *Manhattan Tutors* Guide to the
Primary 4 ISEE®
Mathematics

Manhattan Tutors
office@manhattan-tutors.com

Acknowledgements

Special thanks to:

Meghan Flanigan
Andrea Gottstein
Alex Polizzotti
Meredith Willis
Richard Wu

Contents

Part I
Introduction

How to Use This Book

This book is designed to help students in grade 3 master the Mathematics section of the Primary 4 *Independent School Entrance Exam* (ISEE).

Over the years, the team at Manhattan Tutors has found that students are understandably overwhelmed by the enormous amount of information contained in most test prep books. The math section of the Primary 4 ISEE tends to be particularly intimidating for students who are preparing for the test.

The Manhattan Tutors Guide to the Primary 4 ISEE: Mathematics was written with students in mind. Our streamlined guide is designed to provide students with a tailored study plan that they can use to focus their preparation and minimize the amount of time they need to get ready for the ISEE.

Here's your step-by-step guide for using this book:

1. With your student, read through the Mathematics Strategies in Part II and complete the practice problems.

2. Have your student take the first practice test in Part V. Review the questions he or she answered incorrectly, and focus your remaining time on studying those question types and math fundamentals.

3. Six weeks before the real test, take the second practice test in Part V. Compare your student's results with those from the first practice test, and identify areas of improvement and areas he or she still needs to work on.

4. Four weeks before the real test, take the diagnostic test provided by the ERB. This test, *What to Expect on the Primary 4 ISEE*, can be found at www.erblearn.org/families/isee-preparation.

5. Remember: the ISEE is just one component of a comprehensive application. Schools consider a student's grades, extracurriculars, teacher recommendations, and personal essays, so try not to stress too much over the test!

Warmest regards,

The Staff of Manhattan Tutors

The Primary 4 ISEE: What You Need to Know

The ISEE is a standardized admissions test administered by the Educational Records Bureau (ERB). Many of the independent elementary, middle, and high schools that are members of the ERB require the ISEE, or another standardized test such as the SSAT, as part of their admissions processes.

Test Structure
The ISEE is offered at four levels (primary, lower, middle, and upper), based on the grade to which the student is applying. The Primary 4 ISEE is for students in grade 3 who are applying for admission to grade 4. The test is offered in both online and paper testing formats and is composed of multiple-choice Mathematics and Reading questions. The number of questions and the time allotted for each section can be found in the table below.

Section	Number of Questions	Time Allotted (in minutes)
Reading	28	30
Break		5-10
Mathematics	28	30

The ISEE aligns with national standards in English and Mathematics as articulated in standards adopted by the National Council of Teachers of English and the National Council of Teachers of Mathematics.

Mathematics
Mathematics questions on the Primary 4 ISEE conform to national mathematics standards and ask the student to identify the problem and find a solution to the problem. The questions require one or more cognitive steps in calculating the answer. The questions focus on five categories: number sense and operations, geometric concepts, measurement, algebraic concepts, and data analysis and probability.

Test Logistics

Registering for the ISEE

Students can take the ISEE *once per season*. The Fall, Winter, and Spring / Summer seasons run from August through November, December through March, and April through July, respectively. Most students take the test once in October or November, and again in December, which gives them two shots at the test before the standard January application deadline. You should double-check the website of every school to which you are applying; some schools prefer that students apply earlier in the fall.

The test is offered in-person and online. The most current test dates and locations are found at www.erblearn.org/families/isee-by-erb/

Accommodations

The ISEE offers a wide range of testing accommodations to students with documented learning differences or physical challenges. The process can take up to three weeks, so be sure to submit everything far in advance of when you plan to take the test. Approved accommodations are valid for 15 months from the date of approval. Visit www.erblearn.org/families/isee-accomodations/ for more information.

The Day Before the Test

Don't plan on cramming the day before the test. The most important thing to do is get all necessary items packed up so that you don't forget anything as you're headed out the door!

What to Expect on the Day of the Test

Check www.erblearn.org/families/isee-by-erb/instructions/ to see up-to-date test day instructions. Instructions will vary depending on whether your student is taking the test in-person or online. So that your child may concentrate on doing his or her best on the ISEE, schools do not conduct admission activities or highlight their schools on the day of testing. Knowing that testing may be stressful for some students, schools will provide test administrators who are teachers or other school personnel who teach or interact with children on a daily basis. Test administrators may not discuss test questions during the test. However, they will give clear test directions, and your child is encouraged to ask for clarification, if necessary, before beginning each section of the test. There is one short break following the Reading section. *There is no guessing penalty on the Primary 4 ISEE*, so your student should answer every question on the test!

What to Bring to the Test

The following items are prohibited at all testing centers: cell phones and other electronic devices, calculator watches, rulers, protractors, compasses, dictionaries, and thesauruses. Blank space in the test booklet may be used as scratch paper.

Understanding Your Scores

The ISEE provides perhaps the most baffling score report of any standardized test. Your results will show four scores for both multiple-choice sections of the test: a scaled score, percentile rank, stanine, and stanine analysis. When friends tell you what they scored on the ISEE, they're almost always talking about the stanines. Schools care most about your stanine and percentile rank.

Scaled Score: ranges from 400 to 499 for each section and is derived from your raw score. Your raw score is how many questions you answered correctly on each section. The scaled score has the same meaning regardless of which version of the test was used. The scaled score takes the slight differences between tests into account and allows the ERB to report a score on a common scale that has the same meaning for all students, regardless of the version taken.

Percentile Rank: compares your score in each section to other students in the same grade who have taken the test. A percentile rank of 75, for example, means that you did as well as or better than 75 percent of students in your grade who have taken the Primary 4 ISEE.

Stanine: ranges from 1 to 9 for each section. A score of 1 to 3 is considered below average, 4 to 6 average, and 7 to 9 above average.

Stanine Analysis: Each letter in the stanine analysis box in the Test Profile is the midpoint of a band that extends to either side of the stanine score. The percentile score is an estimate of a student's ability or knowledge. A student's "true score" likely falls within the band reflected by a particular stanine. If the stanine is 5, for example, the percentile rank range is 40-59.

Part II
Mathematics Strategies

Mathematics Strategies

As with all standardized tests, you'll often hear that you must possess a thorough understanding of all the topics on the ISEE in order to do well. While this is what the ERB would like you to believe, it simply isn't true. Learning the math fundamentals tested on the ISEE should of course be one of your top priorities. However, mastering the strategies in this section can help boost your score even higher, and you should always be thinking of them as you move through the mathematics section on the test.

Strategies are listed in order from least difficult to master to most difficult to master. There is a Mini Quiz after each section to help you practice implementing the strategies.

1. Familiarize yourself with the computer test format and test directions

The test administrator will have set up the test for each student's computer station. Do not touch the computer until told to do so. The directions the test administrator will read to you before you begin each section of the Primary 4 ISEE are below. The test will not begin until after the administrator has finished reading the directions and has answered any questions students may have.

Students will be presented with the following directions:

"Read the directions printed at the beginning of each section carefully. Work as quickly as you can without becoming careless. Answer all of the questions that you can. Do not spend too much time on any question that is difficult for you to answer. You may mark questions that you would like to come back to later using the flag icon at the top left of the computer screen. Then, if you have time, use the "Review" button to return to any questions you may have skipped. Try to answer every question, even if you have to guess. On this test, unanswered questions will be counted the same way as wrong answers, so educated guessing is appropriate and may even help you get a higher score. There is no added penalty for an incorrect or unanswered question."

When the test administrator is ready, the student will be directed to start the test.

What to expect on the computer test

According to the ERB, "While most students in this age range today have a good bit of experience with computers, the Primary 4 ISEE does not assume that all students have any particular level of computer skill. Students need only use a few key strokes in order to complete the test. Before the test begins, the administrator conducts a practice section which ensures that students are comfortable with the computer before they begin the test."

It is extremely important that you visit the Primary 4 ISEE section of www.erblearn.org in order to familiarize your student with what the computer screens will look like on the day of the test. The ERB provides five example screens for your reference. Many students who are otherwise well-prepared for the test perform poorly because they are not accustomed to taking a computerized test.

2. Fill in an answer for every question

There is no penalty for guessing on the ISEE, so you have a 25% chance of getting a question correct by randomly choosing A, B, C, or D.

Do not spend too much time on any question that is difficult for you to answer. You may mark questions that you would like to come back to later using the **flag** icon at the top left of the computer screen. Then, if you have time, use the "Review" button to return to any questions you may have skipped. Try to answer every question, even if you have to guess. On this test, unanswered questions will be counted the same way as wrong answers, so educated guessing is appropriate and may even help you get a higher score. There is no added penalty for an incorrect or unanswered question.

Mini Quiz - Strategy #2
Questions: 6
Time Limit: 3 minutes

1. The perimeter of a square is 12s. What is the length of one side?

    (A)   3
    (B)   6
    (C)   3s
    (D)   6s

2. What is the value of x in the math equation $16 = 3x + 4$?

    (A)   1
    (B)   2
    (C)   3
    (D)   4

3. In a warehouse, there are 521 boxes with 12 toys in each box. Which expression gives the best estimate of the total number of toys in the warehouse?

    (A) 50×10
    (B) 52×10
    (C) 500×10
    (D) 600×20

4. What is the value of n in the expression $\frac{20(25 + 35)}{4} = n$?

    (A)   200
    (B)   300
    (C)   400
    (D)   600

5. Which fraction is equivalent to 0.25?

    (A) $\frac{1}{4}$

    (B) $\frac{1}{25}$

    (C) $\frac{25}{25}$

    (D) $\frac{25}{50}$

6. What is the sum of $1.9 + 3.7$?

    (A) $4\frac{3}{5}$

    (B) $5\frac{1}{5}$

    (C) $5\frac{2}{5}$

    (D) $5\frac{3}{5}$

Did you find those questions difficult? That's because several of them were Lower Level ISEE math questions! The time limit was also deliberately decreased on this quiz to force you to select answers quickly. If you applied Strategy #2, you should have still circled an answer for each question. Check the answer key to see how many you guessed correctly!

3. Pay close attention to what the question asks

Some answers might seem correct but don't address what the question asks. The writers of the ISEE are deliberately trying to trick you – don't fall for it! You should get in the habit of paying close attention to key words in the questions so that you don't miss terms such as *positive, negative, sum,* etc. Reading comprehension still plays a huge role in the Primary 4 ISEE Mathematics section.

Example #1

Which positive value of x satisfies the equation $(x + 3)(x - 5) = 0$?

(A)   -5
(B)   -3
(C)   3
(D)   5

This question is more difficult than what you will see on the Primary 4 ISEE. However, by using your reading comprehension skills, you can still eliminate two wrong answer choices. The question specifically asks for a *positive* value. Therefore, you should immediately cross off (A) and (B). **Choice (D) is the only correct answer.**

In the Mini Quiz on the next page, key words are in bold. You should get in the habit of paying attention to similar terms on every Primary 4 ISEE Mathematics question.

Mini Quiz - Strategy #3
Questions: 3
Time Limit: 3 minutes

1. If $x + 4 = 6$, then $2x = $?

    (A)   2
    (B)   3
    (C)   4
    (D)   6

2. If Nicole walks 1 **mile** in 20 **minutes**,
    how many **miles** does she walk in 2
    hours?

    (A)   1
    (B)   6
    (C)   12
    (D)   18

3. The width of a square is 8 inches. What
    is the square's **area**?

    (A)   8 square inches
    (B)   16 square inches
    (C)   32 square inches
    (D)   64 square inches

Make sure you confirm what these questions are asking before you select your answer!

4. Be efficient with your time

You have just over one minute to complete each of the questions on the Mathematics section. If you've been working on a question for 20 seconds and feel like you're stuck, it's time to move on. You can always go back to it later if you have time.

Each question is worth 1 point, regardless of difficulty. If you spend 15 minutes working on 10 impossible questions at the beginning of the section and you end up not having time to do 10 super easy questions at the end of the section, you just got 20 questions wrong! If you'd had time to work on those last 10 questions, you would have gotten 10 correct overall.

Mini Quiz - Strategy #4
Questions: 7
Time Limit: 7 minutes

1. If $4x + 3 = 15$, what is the value of $3x$?

    (A)   3
    (B)   6
    (C)   9
    (D)   12

2. If x can be divided by both 4 and 5 without leaving a remainder, then x can also be divided by which number without leaving a remainder?

    (A)   8
    (B)   12
    (C)   15
    (D)   20

3. Use the set of numbers shown to answer the question.

    $$\{2, 6, 10, 18, 24...\}$$

    Which describes this set of numbers?

    (A)   prime numbers
    (B)   composite numbers
    (C)   even numbers
    (D)   odd numbers

4. $2 + 20 =$

    (A)   2
    (B)   10
    (C)   20
    (D)   22

5. Use the pattern to help answer the question.

    $$1 + 3 = 2^2$$
    $$1 + 3 + 5 = 3^2$$
    $$1 + 3 + 5 + 7 = 4^2$$

    What is the solution to
    $1 + 3 + 5 + 7 + 9 + 11 + 13$?

    (A) 5^2
    (B) 7^2
    (C) 13^2
    (D) 15^2

6. Which of the following is the greatest?

    (A) $6.7 + 4.2$
    (B) $6.7 - 4.2$
    (C) $\frac{6.7}{4.2}$
    (D) 6.7×4.2

7. Which improper fraction is equivalent to $10\frac{1}{2}$?

    (A) $\frac{1}{2}$
    (B) $\frac{5}{2}$
    (C) $\frac{20}{2}$
    (D) $\frac{21}{2}$

Questions 3, 4, 6, and 7 are a bit easier than the others. If you spent too much time on 1, 2, and 5, you may not have had time to attempt the easier questions.

5. Don't fall for trick answers

The ERB claims it doesn't include answers that are intended to trick students, but that's misleading. The ERB acknowledges that it includes *common mistakes or misconceptions* in its answer choices. Although there are some genuinely easy questions on the ISEE, be very careful when choosing your answer.

Example #1
Kayla draws a path on the coordinate grid. She begins at point (1,2) and moves 3 spaces to the right and 4 spaces up.

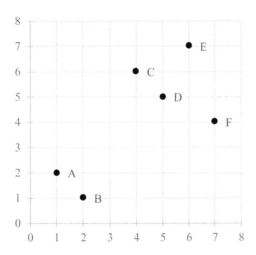

What is the point where Kayla lands?

(A)   *C*
(B)   *D*
(C)   *E*
(D)   *F*

On the coordinate grid, the first number in a pair of points refers to horizontal movement, and the second number refers to vertical movement. To find (1,2), start at (0,0) – also known as the origin – and then move right 1 and up 2. You'll land on point *A*. This is Kayla's starting position. Then, move 3 spaces to the right and 4 spaces up to land on point *C*. **Choice (A) is the correct answer**. If you got mixed up, you might have first gone 2 spaces to the right and 1 space up and landed on point *B* as your starting point. From there, if you went 3 spaces to the right and 4 spaces up, you would have landed on point *D*.

Mini Quiz - Strategy #5
Questions: 4
Time Limit: 4 minutes

1. What fraction of the largest triangle below is shaded in?

   (A) $\frac{4}{5}$

   (B) $\frac{5}{4}$

   (C) $\frac{4}{9}$

   (D) $\frac{9}{4}$

2. Which of the following fractions is equivalent to 0.3?

   (A) $\frac{3}{10}$

   (B) $\frac{3}{100}$

   (C) $\frac{30}{30}$

   (D) $\frac{30}{50}$

3. Brooks draws a path on the coordinate grid. He begins at point (3,1) and moves 3 spaces to the right and 4 spaces up.

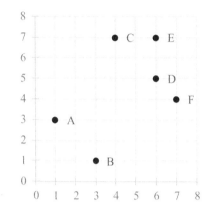

What is the point where Brooks lands?

   (A)   C
   (B)   D
   (C)   E
   (D)   F

4. Which of the following is equivalent to 8?

   (A) $12 \times 4 \div 2$
   (B) $16 \div 4 \times 2$
   (C) $48 \div 3 \times 2$
   (D) $4 \times 5 \div 2$

6. Work backwards

There is one major, helpful difference between the ISEE and the tests you take in school: it's entirely multiple choice. There is exactly one correct answer to each question, and you can use this to your advantage. If you encounter a question you don't know how to solve, try using the answer choices provided by the ISEE to work backwards.

Example #1
If $x + 2 = 10$, what is the value of x?

(A)   5
(B)   6
(C)   7
(D)   8

$5 + 2 = 7$, so (A) is incorrect. $6 + 2 = 8$, so (B) is also incorrect. It's probably pretty obvious to you that (C) doesn't work, either. $8 + 2 = 10$, so you know **(D) is the correct answer.**

Example #2
Dorothy recorded the number of grasshoppers on her front porch each day for five days. She spotted four more grasshoppers on Thursday than she did on Tuesday and Wednesday combined.

GRASSHOPPERS SPOTTED EACH DAY

Monday	🦗🦗🦗🦗
Tuesday	🦗🦗
Wednesday	🦗
Thursday	🦗🦗🦗🦗🦗
Friday	🦗🦗

Based on the data, how many grasshoppers are represented by the 🦗 ?

(A)   1
(B)   2
(C)   3
(D)   4

This question is tricky. You can make it easier by using the given answer choices and working backwards. If (A) is correct, then Dorothy spotted a total of 3 grasshoppers on Tuesday and Wednesday combined and 5 grasshoppers on Thursday. But, 5 is only 2 greater than 3, so this doesn't match what the question says. Now, let's look at (B). If this answer is correct, then Dorothy spotted 6 grasshoppers on Tuesday and Wednesday combined, and 10 grasshoppers on Thursday. 10 is 4 greater than 6, **so (B) is the correct answer!**

Mini Quiz - Strategy #6
Questions: 4
Time Limit: none

1. Isaac recorded the number of hummingbirds at the feeder each day for five days. He spotted five more hummingbirds on Friday than he did on Monday and Thursday combined.

HUMMINGBIRDS SPOTTED EACH DAY

Monday	🦅 🦅
Tuesday	🦅 🦅 🦅
Wednesday	🦅
Thursday	🦅 🦅
Friday	🦅 🦅 🦅 🦅 🦅

Based on the data, how many hummingbirds are represented by the ?

(A)   1
(B)   3
(C)   5
(D)   7

2. If $2x + 1 = 7$, what is the value of x?

(A)   1
(B)   2
(C)   3
(D)   4

3. Lynelle solves a problem using the clue table.

Clue Table

In the equation $\odot + (\blacktriangle \times \star) = 16$, what is the value of $\star$?

(A)   1
(B)   2
(C)   3
(D)   4

4. If $4x - 1 = 19$, what is the value of x?

(A)   5
(B)   6
(C)   7
(D)   8

Working backwards is an advanced strategy that requires a lot of practice, but it's an extremely powerful tool once it's mastered. You can only work backwards when each answer choice is a number.

Answer Key – Mathematics Strategies

Strategy #2
1.   C
2.   D
3.   C
4.   B
5.   A
6.   D

Strategy #3
1.   C
2.   B
3.   D

Strategy #4
1.   C
2.   D
3.   C
4.   D
5.   B
6.   D
7.   D

Strategy #5
1.   C
2.   A
3.   B
4.   B

Strategy #6
1.   C
2.   C
3.   D
4.   A

Part III
Mathematics Fundamentals

Math Definitions

You must memorize the following definitions before taking the Primary 4 ISEE.

Vocab Word	Definition	Examples
Integer	A number that does not contain fractions or decimals Integers can be positive, negative, or zero	-100, -5, 0, 2, 50
Even number	A number that is divisible by two. Zero is even	-34, -10, 0, 8, 92
Odd number	A number that is not divisible by two	-7, 1, 9, 45
Positive number	A number greater than zero	1, 4, 45, 100
Negative number	A number less than zero	-34, -16, -9, -5
Whole number	Positive integers and zero	0, 1, 5, 50, 75
Divisible by	A number is divisible by another if the remainder after division is zero	10 is divisible by 2 7 is not divisible by 2
Factor	All of the integers that a certain integer is divisible by Each integer has limited factors	The factors of 20 are 1, 2, 4, 5, 10, and 20
Multiple	The result of multiplying an integer by another integer Each integer has infinite multiples	Multiples of 5 include 5, 10, 15, 20, 25, etc
Prime number	A number divisible only by 1 and itself. 1 is not prime 2 is the only even prime number	2, 3, 5, 7, 11, 13, 17
Composite number	A whole number that has more than two factors	4, 6, 9, 21, 100
Consecutive numbers	A series of integers that appear in the same order as they do on the number line	5, 6, 7 -6, -5, -4
Distinct numbers	Numbers that are different from one another	1, 2, 3, 4, 5
Sum	The result of addition	The sum of 5 and 7 is 12
Difference	The result of subtraction	The difference of 20 and 5 is 15
Product	The result of multiplication	The product of 3 and 9 is 27
Quotient	The result of division	The quotient of 12 and 4 is 3
Remainder	The amount that is left over after performing division	When 9 is divided by 2, the remainder is 1
Inclusive	Includes all integers in a range	There are 5 integers, inclusive, from 7 to 11 (7, 8, 9, 10, and 11)

Digits	The integers from 0 to 9	123 has three digits
Numerator	The top part of a fraction	The numerator of $\frac{4}{5}$ is 4
Denominator	The bottom part of a fraction	The denominator of $\frac{10}{13}$ is 13

Practice Problems

1. List 5 integers
2. List 5 prime numbers
3. Is 1 prime?
4. Is 2 prime?
5. List 4 consecutive integers
6. What is the quotient of 100 and 5?
7. List 5 multiples of 4
8. How many digits does 109,805 have?
9. When 100 is divided by 30, what is the remainder?
10. What is the denominator of $\frac{7}{15}$?

11. List 5 composite numbers
12. What is the product of 5 and 8?
13. What is the sum of 12 and 22?
14. What are all the factors of 16?
15. List 5 multiples of 3
16. Is 0 even or odd?
17. Is 20 divisible by 3?
18. What is the sum of the digits from 8 to 11, inclusive?
19. Is -5 a whole number?
20. Is 0 an integer?

Order of Operations / PEMDAS

The order of operations (PEMDAS) tells you in what order you must solve equations. You may already be familiar with the trick for remembering PEMDAS:

Please Excuse My Dear Aunt Sally

This means that you should always complete **p**arentheses first, then **e**xponents. **M**ultiplication and **d**ivision are then completed from left to right; finally, **a**ddition and **s**ubtraction are completed from left to right.

Correct: $12 - 5 + 3 = 7 + 3 = 10$ ✓

Incorrect: $12 - 5 + 3 = 12 - 8 = 4$ ✗

Correct: $14 \div 7 + 10 \times 4 - 6 + 5 = 2 + 40 - 6 + 5 = 42 - 6 + 5 = 36 + 5 = 41$ ✓

Incorrect: $14 \div 7 + 10 \times 4 - 6 + 5 = 2 + 40 - 6 + 5 = 42 - 6 + 5 = 42 - 11 = 31$ ✗

It is very easy to make careless mistakes when working with PEMDAS. To minimize the risk of errors, you can use the inverted pyramid method of solving PEMDAS problems: only simplify one type of operation per line, and then rewrite the simplified equation on the next line. Repeat as necessary until you have simplified the expression.

Example
What is the value of
$(4 - 2) + (5 + 23) + 33 - 6$?
(A)   57
(B)   60
(C)   63
(D)   66

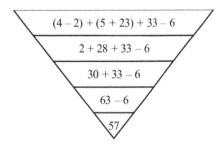

The correct answer is (A).

Example
What is the value of
$10 \div 2 + 3 \times 3 - 4 + 1$?
(A)   11
(B)   18
(C)   21
(D)   30

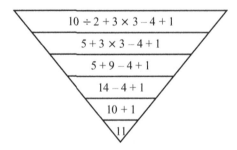

The correct answer is (A).

Practice Problems

1.　　　$15 - 5 + 8 = $ ____
2.　　　$14 + 12 - 6 + 2 = $ ____
3.　　　$2 + (5 - 3) + 4 = $ ____
4.　　　$5 + (9 - 4) + 7 = $ ____
5.　　　$(6 + 2) + (6 - 3) + 1 = $ ____

6.　　　$4 \times 4 - 6 \times 2 = $ ____
7.　　　$3 \times (5 - 2) \div 9 = $ ____
8.　　　$100 \div (20 \div 4 \times 2) = $ ____
9.　　　$6 \times (2 + 7) \div (3 \times 3) \times (2 + 4) = $ ____
10.　　$4 + (2 \times 3) \div (4 \div 2) = $ ____

Introduction to Fractions

Fractions are numerical quantities that are not whole numbers. They are represented in two parts: the numerator (the top) and the denominator (the bottom). Fractions indicate "part out of whole." Examples of fractions include $\frac{1}{2}$ and $\frac{16}{5}$. Fractions also indicate division. $\frac{1}{2}$, for example, means "one divided by two."

Visualizing Fractions
When first learning fractions, it is easiest to use shaded shapes to visualize them.

Example
What fraction is represented by the shaded section of the shape below?

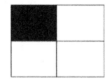

The square is divided into 4 equal sections, and 1 section is shaded in. Remember, fractions indicate "part out of whole." What *part* of the *whole* shape is shaded in? 1 part out of 4. You can represent this fraction as $\frac{1}{4}$

Something very important to note about the shape above is that *it was divided into 4 sections of equal size.* You cannot make a fraction out of one shape that has been divided into sections of different sizes. However, it is possible to say what fraction of a total number of shapes are shaded in, even if they are not all the same size.

Example
What fraction is represented by the unshaded section of the shape below?

There are 2 unshaded sections, and a total of 5 equally sized sections. Therefore, the unshaded sections represent the fraction $\frac{2}{5}$

Visualizing Equivalent Fractions

Fractions that look different, like $\frac{1}{2}$ and $\frac{2}{4}$, can mean the same thing.

Example

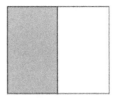   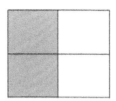   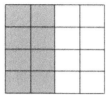

Above, you can see three large squares of equal size that have all been divided into a different number of equally sized smaller pieces. The first square is divided into 2 pieces, the second square is divided into 4 pieces, and the third square is divided into 16 pieces. Furthermore, an equally sized section of each of the larger squares has been shaded in.

The first square represents the fraction $\frac{1}{2}$: one piece out of two equally sized pieces has been shaded in.

The second square represents the fraction $\frac{2}{4}$: two pieces out of four equally sized pieces have been shaded in. Finally, the third square represents $\frac{8}{16}$: eight pieces out of sixteen equally sized pieces have been shaded in.

Visually, you can see that the same total amount of each square has been shaded. That means that

$$\frac{1}{2} = \frac{2}{4} = \frac{8}{16}$$

Example

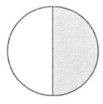   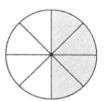

Above, you can see two circles of equal size that have been divided into a different number of equally sized pieces. The circle on the left represents the fraction $\frac{1}{2}$. The circle on the right represents the fraction $\frac{4}{8}$. When you look at the circles, you can see that the same portion of each one has been shaded in. Therefore, $\frac{1}{2} = \frac{4}{8}$

Reducing Fractions

To reduce a fraction, figure out a number that the top and bottom of the fraction are both divisible by. For example, if both numbers in the fraction are even, you can start by dividing by 2.

Example

Reduce the fraction $\frac{8}{10}$

8 and 10 are both even, so you can divide both of them by 2. $\frac{8 \div 2}{10 \div 2} = \frac{4}{5}$. This fraction can't be reduced any further. $\frac{8}{10} = \frac{4}{5}$. Both will result in 0.8 if you plug them into a calculator.

If the numbers on the top and the bottom of the fraction are not both even, you'll have to think of a number other than 2 that they are both divisible by.

Example

Reduce the fraction $\frac{15}{25}$

2 does not go into 15 or 25, but 5 goes into both numbers. Divide both numbers by 5.

$\frac{15 \div 5}{25 \div 5} = \frac{3}{5}$. There are no numbers that go into both 3 and 5, so this fraction has been reduced as much as possible.

Example

Reduce the fraction $\frac{27}{81}$

Although 27 and 81 are not even, you might notice that they are both divisible by 9.

$\frac{27 \div 9}{81 \div 9} = \frac{3}{9}$. You're not finished just yet: 3 and 9 are both divisible by 3.

$\frac{3 \div 3}{9 \div 3} = \frac{1}{3}$. This fraction is now fully reduced.

Practice Problems

Fully Reduce

1. $\dfrac{10}{20}$

2. $\dfrac{6}{10}$

3. $\dfrac{15}{45}$

4. $\dfrac{999}{999}$

5. $\dfrac{232}{444}$

6. $\dfrac{55}{99}$

7. $\dfrac{100}{300}$

8. $\dfrac{126}{94}$

9. $\dfrac{12}{9}$

10. $\dfrac{20}{10}$

11. $\dfrac{32}{34}$

12. $\dfrac{7}{35}$

13. $\dfrac{10}{100}$

14. $\dfrac{8}{24}$

15. $\dfrac{15}{30}$

16. $\dfrac{5}{40}$

17. $\dfrac{20}{60}$

18. $\dfrac{40}{50}$

19. $\dfrac{18}{45}$

20. $\dfrac{12}{18}$

Improper Fractions and Mixed Numbers

So far, we have dealt only with fractions in which the numerator is smaller than the denominator. In many instances, however, the numerator will be larger than the denominator. This type of fraction is known as an "improper fraction." Because fractions indicate division, this means that improper fractions represent numbers larger than 1. $\frac{9}{4}$ means "9 divided by 4." While you might not know the exact value off the top of your head, you do know that 4 goes into 9 more than one time.

You will need to know how to convert between improper fractions and mixed numbers. Mixed numbers are another way of representing improper fractions. To convert an improper fraction into a mixed number, see how many times the denominator of the fraction goes evenly into the numerator of the fraction. That result goes on the left. Then, take whatever is left over (the remainder) and put it over what was originally the denominator of the fraction. This fraction goes on the right.

Example

Convert $\frac{9}{7}$ to a mixed number

7 goes into 9 one time, with a remainder of 2. Place the 1 on the left, then take the remaining 2 and put it on top of your original denominator, which gives you $1\frac{2}{7}$

Example

Convert $\frac{30}{11}$ to a mixed number

11 goes into 30 two times, with a remainder of 8. Put the 2 on the left and the 8 on top of the original denominator. The final answer is $2\frac{8}{11}$

To convert from a mixed number to an improper fraction, multiply the denominator of the fraction by the big number on the left. Then, add the numerator of the fraction to this number. This sum becomes the new numerator, while the original denominator remains the same.

Example

Convert $3\frac{4}{9}$ to an improper fraction

$9 \times 3 = 27$, and $27 + 4 = 31$. 31 is the new numerator, and the denominator is 9. The improper fraction is $\frac{31}{9}$

Representing Fractions as Whole Numbers

Fractions represent division. Therefore, $\frac{15}{1} = 15$, $\frac{40}{1} = 40$, etc.

Example
What fraction of the circle below is shaded in?

You can see that the whole fraction is shaded in, so in most cases 1 would be an acceptable answer. However, this question asks you to represent your answer as a fraction. There are 4 pieces, and all 4 pieces are shaded in, so the fraction is $\frac{4}{4}$

Example
What fraction of the circles below is shaded in?

In most cases, 2 would be an acceptable answer. Once again, you've been asked to give your answer as a fraction. Each circle has been divided into 2 pieces, and 4 pieces total have been shaded in, so the answer is $\frac{4}{2}$

Practice Problems

Convert to Mixed Numbers

1. $\frac{9}{4}$

2. $\frac{12}{5}$

3. $\frac{99}{80}$

4. $\frac{50}{40}$

5. $\frac{27}{4}$

6. $\frac{17}{16}$

7. $\frac{3}{2}$

8. $\frac{88}{45}$

Convert to Improper Fractions

9. $1\frac{2}{7}$

10. $2\frac{3}{4}$

11. $1\frac{5}{12}$

12. $4\frac{3}{8}$

13. $3\frac{4}{9}$

14. $5\frac{1}{5}$

15. $4\frac{2}{3}$

16. $8\frac{8}{9}$

Convert to Whole Numbers

17. $\frac{4}{2}$

18. $\frac{100}{10}$

19. $\frac{12}{3}$

20. $\frac{5}{5}$

21. $\frac{27}{9}$

Operations with Fractions

In this section, you will learn to add, subtract, multiply, divide, and compare fractions. You will also learn strategies for questions that involve adding or subtracting mixed numbers.

Adding and Subtracting Fractions

Adding and subtracting fractions requires a common denominator. That means the denominator of both fractions must be the same number. When you add or subtract the fractions, only the numerators will change.

Example

$$\frac{6}{11} + \frac{4}{11} = \frac{10}{11}$$

If the bottoms of the fractions are not the same, you have to do more work. You must ask yourself what number both of the denominators go into.

Example

$$\frac{3}{7} + \frac{1}{2} = ?$$

7 and 2 both go into 14. For $\frac{3}{7}$, $7 \times 2 = 14$, so you'll also need to multiply the numerator by 2, giving you $\frac{3 \times 2}{7 \times 2} = \frac{6}{14}$. For $\frac{1}{2}$, $2 \times 7 = 14$, so you'll also need to multiply 1 by 7, giving you $\frac{1 \times 7}{2 \times 7} = \frac{7}{14}$. Now that you've found a common denominator, you can add like you did in the first example. $\frac{3}{7} + \frac{1}{2} = \frac{6}{14} + \frac{7}{14} = \frac{13}{14}$

Sometimes, it can be tricky to find a common denominator. Using the *bow tie method* will help you easily find a common denominator in any pair of fractions!

Example

$$\frac{1}{7} + \frac{4}{9} = ?$$

Although you might have a hard time finding the common multiple of 7 and 9, you can easily solve this equation by using the bow tie method. $9 \times 1 = 9$, $7 \times 4 = 28$, and $7 \times 9 = 63$. You can rewrite this equation as $\frac{9}{63} + \frac{28}{63} = \frac{37}{63}$

Multiplying and Dividing Fractions

Multiplying and dividing fractions is much easier than adding and subtracting fractions! When multiplying, simply multiply straight across the numerator and straight across the denominator.

Example

$$\frac{6}{11} \times \frac{4}{11} = ?$$

$$\frac{6}{11} \times \frac{4}{11} = \frac{6 \times 4}{11 \times 11} = \frac{24}{121}$$

Dividing fractions requires two more steps than multiplying fractions. First, flip the second fraction. Then, change the division sign to multiplication and multiply like you did in the previous example. This method is called "keep, switch, flip," because you "keep" the first fraction, "switch" the division sign, and "flip" the second fraction.

Example

$$\frac{6}{11} \div \frac{4}{11} = ?$$

$$\frac{6}{11} \div \frac{4}{11} = \frac{6}{11} \times \frac{11}{4} = \frac{6 \times 11}{11 \times 4} = \frac{66}{44} = \frac{33}{22} = \frac{3}{2}$$

Finally, you should know that any fraction that has a 0 in the denominator is *undefined*. Fractions like $\frac{0}{0}$ or $\frac{19}{0}$ cannot be solved. Fractions with 0 in the numerator and any number except 0 in the denominator equal 0. For example, $\frac{0}{10} = 0$.

Comparing Fractions

You may be asked to compare fractions. Using a partial bowtie method makes this a piece of cake!

Example

Which is larger: $\frac{2}{11}$ or $\frac{3}{20}$?

$$\frac{2}{11} \div \frac{3}{20} = \overset{40}{\underset{}{\frac{2}{11}}} \times \overset{33}{\underset{}{\frac{3}{20}}}$$

Multiply the denominator of one fraction by the numerator of the other fraction, and then write the product above the numerator. Whichever fraction has the larger number above it is the larger fraction. In this case, $\frac{2}{11} > \frac{3}{20}$ because 40 > 33.

You might be asked which fraction is the least of four fractions like $\frac{6}{10}, \frac{9}{20}, \frac{21}{40},$ and $\frac{25}{50}$. You may be able to see that only one of the fractions, $\frac{9}{20}$, is less than $\frac{1}{2}$, so you do not need to use the method shown above.

Adding and Subtracting Mixed Numbers

Finally, you may tested on how to add and subtract simple mixed numbers. This is an advanced topic for 3rd graders; rather than learn the "correct" method, we recommend you use some logic and common sense when solving these questions.

Example

Jordan has a bowl of fruit that weighs 11 pounds in total. The bowl holding the fruit weighs $1\frac{1}{4}$ pounds. How much does the fruit weigh?

(A) $8\frac{3}{4}$ pounds

(B) $9\frac{3}{4}$ pounds

(C) $10\frac{1}{4}$ pounds

(D) $10\frac{3}{4}$ pounds

Think of it this way: if the bowl weighed 1 pound, the fruit would weigh $11 - 1 = 10$ pounds. If the bowl weighed 2 pounds, then the fruit would weigh $11 - 2 = 9$ pounds. Because the actual weight of the bowl is between 1 and 2 pounds, then then actual weight of the fruit will be between 9 and 10 pounds. **The only answer choice that works is (B).** As you can see, you can use the multiple-choice format of the test to your advantage on questions like these.

Example

Jessie is collecting sand to build a sandcastle. Her bucket of sand weighs 17 pounds. The bucket holding the sand weighs $3\frac{3}{4}$ pounds. How much does the sand weigh?

(A) $13\frac{1}{4}$ pounds

(B) $13\frac{3}{4}$ pounds

(C) $14\frac{1}{4}$ pounds

(D) $14\frac{3}{4}$ pounds

Once again, use common sense: $3\frac{3}{4}$ is very close to 4.

$17 - 4 = 13$, so the correct answer will be the one that is closest to 13. **(A) is the correct answer.**

Practice Problems

Add, Subtract, Multiply, or Divide

1. $\dfrac{5}{9} + \dfrac{2}{9} =$ _____

2. $\dfrac{5}{11} \div \dfrac{4}{9} =$ _____

3. $\dfrac{3}{7} \times \dfrac{6}{7} =$ _____

4. $\dfrac{11}{12} - \dfrac{3}{4} =$ _____

5. $\dfrac{19}{20} \div \dfrac{2}{3} =$ _____

6. $\dfrac{23}{25} + \dfrac{1}{5} =$ _____

7. $\dfrac{8}{13} - \dfrac{4}{13} =$ _____

8. $\dfrac{7}{8} - \dfrac{1}{2} =$ _____

9. $\dfrac{9}{11} \div \dfrac{3}{4} =$ _____

10. $\dfrac{2}{9} \times \dfrac{3}{7} =$ _____

Which Fraction is Larger?

11. $\dfrac{2}{7}$ *or* $\dfrac{3}{8}$

12. $\dfrac{3}{4}$ *or* $\dfrac{7}{10}$

13. $\dfrac{1}{6}$ *or* $\dfrac{1}{7}$

14. $\dfrac{4}{5}$ *or* $\dfrac{8}{10}$

15. $\dfrac{7}{12}$ *or* $\dfrac{6}{8}$

Solve

16. A boy has a bowl of fruit that weighs 9 pounds in total. The bowl holding the fruit weighs $2\dfrac{3}{4}$ pounds. How much does the fruit weigh?

   (A) $5\dfrac{3}{4}$ pounds

   (B) $6\dfrac{1}{4}$ pounds

   (C) $6\dfrac{3}{4}$ pounds

   (D) $7\dfrac{1}{4}$ pounds

17. A girl is collecting sand to build a sandcastle. Her bucket of sand weighs 13 pounds. The bucket holding the sand weighs $2\dfrac{1}{2}$ pounds. How much does the sand weigh?

   (A) $10\dfrac{1}{2}$ pounds

   (B)   11 pounds

   (C) $11\dfrac{1}{4}$ pounds

   (D) $11\dfrac{1}{2}$ pounds

18. Jimmy is carrying a box of books home that weighs 16 pounds in total. The books weigh $14\frac{3}{4}$ pounds. How much does the box weigh?

    (A) $\frac{3}{4}$ of a pound

    (B)   1 pound

    (C) $1\frac{1}{4}$ pounds

    (D) $1\frac{3}{4}$ pounds

19. Raine keeps her collection of spare change in a box. Her collection weighs 4 pounds in total. If the coins weigh $3\frac{3}{4}$ pounds, how much does the box weigh?

    (A) $\frac{1}{4}$ of a pound

    (B) $\frac{1}{2}$ of a pound

    (C) $\frac{3}{4}$ of a pound

    (D)   1 pound

20. A boy is building a sandcastle. His bucket of sand weighs 17 pounds total. The sand weighs $13\frac{1}{4}$ pounds. How much does the bucket weigh?

    (A) $2\frac{1}{4}$ pounds

    (B) $2\frac{3}{4}$ pounds

    (C) $3\frac{1}{4}$ pounds

    (D) $3\frac{3}{4}$ pounds

21. A cart of groceries weighs 48 pounds. If the cart weighs $14\frac{3}{4}$ pounds, how much do the groceries weigh?

    (A) $32\frac{1}{4}$ pounds

    (B) $32\frac{3}{4}$ pounds

    (C) $33\frac{1}{4}$ pounds

    (D) $33\frac{1}{2}$ pounds

22. The combined weight of a couch and a person sitting on the couch is 234 pounds. If the person weighs $149\frac{3}{4}$ pounds, how much does the couch weigh?

    (A) $83\frac{1}{4}$ pounds

    (B) $83\frac{3}{4}$ pounds

    (C) $84\frac{1}{4}$ pounds

    (D) $84\frac{3}{4}$ pounds

Decimals

You will need to be able to add, subtract, and convert decimals on the Primary 4 ISEE.

Adding and Subtracting Decimals

To add and subtract decimals, line up the decimal points and then add or subtract as you normally would.

$$
\begin{array}{r}
17.670 \\
+\ 4.321 \\
\hline
21.991
\end{array}
\qquad\qquad
\begin{array}{r}
9.0100 \\
-\ .0221 \\
\hline
8.9879
\end{array}
$$

Converting Fractions to Decimals

It's easiest to convert fractions to decimals when the denominator of the fraction is 100.

$$\frac{50}{100} = 0.50 \qquad \frac{99}{100} = 0.99 \qquad \frac{36}{100} = 0.36 \qquad \frac{8}{100} = 0.08$$

Notice that all you need to do is move the decimal place in the numerator of the fraction two places to the left in order to create a decimal.

What do you do if the number in the bottom of the fraction is not 100? Use multiplication to change it into 100!

$$\frac{4}{25} = \frac{4 \times 4}{25 \times 4} = \frac{16}{100} = 0.16 \qquad \frac{9}{10} = \frac{9 \times 10}{10 \times 10} = \frac{90}{100} = 0.90 \qquad \frac{1}{50} = \frac{1 \times 2}{50 \times 2} = \frac{2}{100} = 0.02$$

Converting Decimals to Fractions

This is pretty easy: when you are given a decimal, move the decimal two places to the right, put that number in a fraction over 100, and reduce if necessary.

$$0.73 = \frac{73}{100} \qquad 0.42 = \frac{42}{100} = \frac{21}{50} \qquad 0.01 = \frac{1}{100} \qquad 0.12 = \frac{12}{100} = \frac{3}{25}$$

Practice Problems

1. $4.954 - 2.91 = $ _____
2. $3.21 + 0.1202 = $ _____
3. $11.43 - 5.921 = $ _____
4. $12.5 + 6.34 = $ _____
5. $0.491 - 0.199 = $ _____
6. $10.9 + 0.04 = $ _____
7. $4.09 + 6.112 = $ _____
8. $1.2304 - 0.503 = $ _____
9. Convert 0.55 to a fraction
10. Convert 0.09 to a fraction
11. Convert 0.40 to a fraction
12. Convert 0.12 to a fraction

13. Convert 0.95 to a fraction

14. Convert $\frac{43}{100}$ to a decimal

15. Convert $\frac{6}{100}$ to a decimal

16. Convert $\frac{93}{100}$ to a decimal

17. Convert $\frac{1}{100}$ to a decimal

18. Convert $\frac{55}{100}$ to a decimal

Percents

Percent means "out of 100." When you are asked to find a percent, it's the same thing as finding how many times out of 100 times something happens. Once you've mastered fractions and decimals, dealing with percents is easy.

Converting Fractions into Percents

It's easiest to convert fractions into percents when the denominator of the fraction is 100.

$$\frac{50}{100} = 50\% \qquad\qquad \frac{97}{100} = 97\% \qquad\qquad \frac{1}{100} = 1\%$$

If the denominator of the fraction is not 100, you'll need to multiply in order to change it to 100.

$$\frac{10}{25} = \frac{10 \times 4}{25 \times 4} = \frac{40}{100} = 40\% \qquad\qquad \frac{7}{10} = \frac{7 \times 10}{10 \times 10} = \frac{70}{100} = 70\%$$

Converting Percents into Fractions

Converting percents into fractions is also very easy. Drop the percent sign and put the number on the top of a fraction. The denominator of the fraction will always be 100. Then, reduce the fraction if necessary.

$$35\% = \frac{35}{100} = \frac{7}{20} \qquad\qquad 8\% = \frac{8}{100} = \frac{2}{25} \qquad\qquad 99\% = \frac{99}{100}$$

Practice Problems

Convert the Fractions to Percents

1. $\frac{14}{100}$

2. $\frac{65}{100}$

3. $\frac{1}{2}$

4. $\frac{45}{50}$

5. $\frac{8}{10}$

6. $\frac{3}{4}$

Convert the Percents to Decimals

7. 90%
8. 65%
9. 3%
10. 12%

Convert the Percents to Fractions

11. 15%
12. 28%
13. 63%
14. 44%

Units of Measurement

You should memorize the following units of measurement before taking the Primary 4 ISEE. Related questions on the test most often ask for the appropriate units of measurement for a specific item.

Length

Standard unit of measure:

meter

1 meter is approximately 3 feet.

Related units:

Millimeter – about thickness of a credit card
Centimeter – about the length of a staple
Kilometer – a bit more than half a mile

Mass

Standard unit of measure:

gram

1 gram is approximately the weight of a sugar packet

Related units:

Milligram – about the weight of a grain of sand
Kilogram – a little more than two pounds

Volume

Standard unit of measure:

liter

Large bottles of soda are 2 liters

Related units:

Milliliter – about 20 drops of water

Prefixes

You may have noticed that the related units above all use the same prefixes.

Milli: one thousandth
Centi: one hundredth
Kilo: one thousand

Memorizing these prefixes will help you recognize any units of measurement that appear on the ISEE.

Practice Problems

1. What units are most appropriate for measuring the length of a leaf?
2. What units are most appropriate for measuring the weight of a basketball?
3. What units are most appropriate for measuring the volume of a small bottle of medicine?
4. What units are most appropriate for measuring the volume of a bathtub?
5. What units are most appropriate for measuring the weight of a car?
6. What units are most appropriate for measuring the length of a basketball court?
7. What units are most appropriate for measuring the weight of a person?
8. What units are most appropriate for measuring the length of a credit card?

Shapes

You will need to know the names of shapes up to 10 sides on the Primary 4 ISEE.

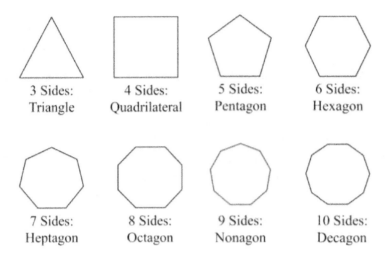

The shapes shown above are all *regular* shapes. That means they have sides that are all equal and interior (inside) angles that are all equal.

Irregular shapes have sides and angles of any length and size. Examples of irregular shapes are given below.

Note that irregular shapes are still named according to the number of sides they have.

Practice Problems

1. A family is building a pool in the shape of a nonagon. How many sides will the pool have?

2. What shape has six sides?

3. How many total sides are there in a hexagon and a heptagon?

4. An octagon is a shape with how many sides?

5. A mosaic is made of hundreds of tiny tiles that each have seven sides. What type of shape are the tiles?

6. A coin has ten sides. What shape is the coin?

7. How many total sides are there in a nonagon and an octagon?

8. Which shape has more sides: a pentagon or a heptagon?

9. What is the length of one side of a regular pentagon with a perimeter of 25 centimeters?

10. What is the length of one side of a regular octagon with a perimeter of 64 inches?

11. The length of one side of a regular heptagon is 7 inches. What is the perimeter of the heptagon?

12. The length of one side of a regular nonagon is 3 meters. What is the perimeter of the nonagon?

13. What is the length of one side of a regular decagon with a perimeter of 120 centimeters?

14. The length of one side of a regular hexagon is 7 inches. What is the hexagon's perimeter?

15. How many total sides are there in a pentagon and a decagon?

16. A regular hexagon has side lengths of 5 inches. If each of the side lengths of the hexagon is doubled, what is the perimeter of the new hexagon?

17. A decagon is a shape with how many sides?

18. Which shape has the greater perimeter: a regular hexagon with side lengths of 7 inches or a regular octagon with side lengths of 5 inches?

19. List the names of shapes in order, starting with a shape that has three sides and going until a shape that has ten sides.

20. What does it mean when a shape is *regular*?

21. How many total sides are there in a pentagon, a hexagon, and an octagon?

Perimeter and Area

Perimeter measures the length of the outside of a shape, while area measures the space inside of a shape.

Perimeter
To find perimeter, add up the lengths of all sides of a shape.

The easiest questions will provide you with all the lengths.

Example
What is the perimeter of the triangle shown below?

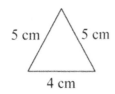

(A)   4 cm
(B)   5 cm
(C)   9 cm
(D)   14 cm

$5 + 5 + 4 = 14$, so **the correct answer is (D).**

Harder questions will only provide some of the side lengths.

Example
What is the perimeter of the rectangle shown below?

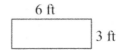

(A)   3 ft
(B)   6 ft
(C)   9 ft
(D)   18 ft

The side across from 3 ft is also equal to 3 ft. The side across from 6 ft is also equal to 6 ft. $3 + 3 + 6 + 6 = 18$. **The correct answer is (D).**

Area
On the Primary 4 ISEE, you will only be asked to find the area of squares and rectangles. To find the area of a square or rectangle, multiply the length by the width. Area is labeled in "square units."

Example
What is the area of the rectangle shown below?

(A)   10 square centimeters
(B)   14 square centimeters
(C)   16 square centimeters
(D)   20 square centimeters

$8 \times 2 = 16$. **The correct answer is (C).**

Example
What is the area of a square with a side length of 5 inches?

(A)   5 square inches
(B)   10 square inches
(C)   20 square inches
(D)   25 square inches

The lengths of all four sides of a square are equal. $5 \times 5 = 25$. **The correct answer is (D).**

Practice Problems

1. What is the area of a square with a side length of 6 centimeters?

2. What is the perimeter of the regular pentagon shown below?

4 in

3. What is the area of a rectangle with a width of 4 feet and a length of 12 feet?

4. What is the perimeter of the shape shown below?

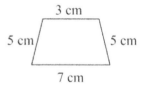

3 cm

5 cm   5 cm

7 cm

5. What is the perimeter of a rectangle with a width of 6 feet and a length of 4 feet?

6. Each square in the shape shown below has an area of 4 square centimeters. What is the shape's total area?

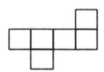

7. What is the perimeter of a regular hexagon with side lengths equal to 5 meters?

8. Each square in the figure below has a perimeter of 12 inches. What is the total perimeter of the 5 shaded squares in the figure?

9. What is the perimeter of a triangle with three equal sides of 3 inches each?

10. What is the width of a rectangle with an area of 45 square feet and a length of 5 feet?

11. What is the perimeter of a square with an area of 25 square centimeters?

12. If each of the side lengths of the triangle below were doubled, what would be the perimeter of the triangle?

5 cm   5 cm

4 cm

13. What is the area of the rectangle shown below?

6 ft

3 ft

14. The side length of a square is 3 inches. Is the square's area or perimeter greater?

15. What is the perimeter of a triangle with side lengths that each measure 12 inches?

Mathematical Properties

There are four mathematical properties you should memorize for the Primary 4 ISEE.

Associative Property

The *associative property* states that when adding or multiplying, the sum or product will be the same regardless of how the numbers are grouped.

Examples

$$2 + 7 + 5 = 2 + 7 + 5 \qquad\qquad 3 \times 4 \times 2 = 3 \times 4 \times 2$$
$$(2 + 7) + 5 = 2 + (7 + 5) \qquad\qquad (3 \times 4) \times 2 = 3 \times (4 \times 2)$$
$$9 + 5 = 2 + 12 \qquad\qquad 12 \times 2 = 3 \times 8$$
$$14 = 14 \qquad\qquad 24 = 24$$

The associative property does not work with subtraction or division.

Commutative Property

The *commutative property* states that you can reverse the order of numbers in addition and multiplication and still get the same answer.

Examples

$$3 + 6 = 6 + 3 \qquad\qquad 3 \times 6 = 6 \times 3$$
$$9 = 9 \qquad\qquad 18 = 18$$

The commutative property does not work with subtraction or division.

Distributive Property

The *distributive property* states that multiplying a number by the sum of two or more numbers is the same as multiplying each number in the sum separately and then adding the products together.

Examples

$$3 \times (2 + 4) = 3 \times 2 + 3 \times 4 \qquad\qquad (4 + 5) \times 3 = 4 \times 3 + 5 \times 3$$
$$3 \times 6 = 6 + 12 \qquad\qquad 9 \times 3 = 12 + 15$$
$$18 = 18 \qquad\qquad 27 = 27$$

Identity Property

The *identity property* states that any number multiplied by 1 is itself.

Examples

$$6 \times 1 = 6 \qquad\qquad 99 \times 1 = 99$$

Practice Problems

Describe Which Property Is Shown

1. $10 \times 1 = 10$

2. $6 \times 2 = 2 \times 6$

3. $1 \times 1 = 1$

4. $(4 \times 8) \times 6 = 4 \times (8 \times 6)$

5. $(8 \times 10) + (8 \times 2) = 8 \times (10 + 2)$

6. $1 \times 7 = 7$

7. $(9 \times 6) \times 7 = 9 \times (6 \times 7)$

8. $3 + 9 = 9 + 3$

9. $4 \times (5 + 7) = 4 \times 5 + 4 \times 7$

10. $12 + 4 + 2 = 2 + 4 + 12$

Quadrilaterals

A quadrilateral is a four-sided shape. There are six special quadrilaterals that you must be familiar with on the Primary 4 ISEE.

There are a few definitions you'll need to know before learning about special quadrilaterals:

Right Angle: a 90-degree angle formed by the intersection of two perpendicular lines
Perpendicular lines: two lines that intersect at 90-degree angles
Parallel lines: a pair of lines that have the same distance continuously between them and never intersect

In the following six figures, the small squares that appear when two sides connect indicate a 90-degree angle.

Squares

A *square* is a quadrilateral with four equal sides and four right angles. Opposite sides are parallel.

- Perimeter = $4s$ = the sum of all four sides
- Area = $s \times s$
- Squares are always rectangles, parallelograms, rhombi, and kites. In other words, squares are a subset of rectangles, parallelograms, rhombi, and kites

Rectangles

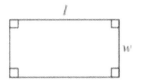

A *rectangle* is a quadrilateral with two pairs of equal sides and four right angles. Opposite sides are parallel.

- Opposite sides are equal
- Perimeter = $2l + 2w$ = the sum of all four sides
- Area = $l \times w$
- A rectangle is a square if all of its sides are the same length. Rectangles are always parallelograms. In other words, rectangles are a subset of parallelograms

Parallelograms

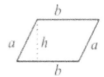

A *parallelogram* is a quadrilateral with two pairs of parallel sides.

- Opposite sides are equal
- Opposite angles are equal
- Parallelograms are rectangles if they contain four right angles. Parallelograms are squares if they contain four right angles and all four sides are the same length. Parallelograms are rhombi if all four sides are the same length

Rhombi or Diamonds*

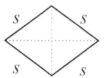

A *rhombus* (plural: *rhombi*), or *diamond*, is a quadrilateral with four equal sides and two pairs of parallel sides.

- Perimeter = 4s = the sum of all four sides
- Opposite angles are equal
- A rhombus is always a parallelogram
- A rhombus is a rectangle and a square if it has four right angles

Kites

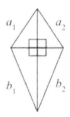

A *kite* is a quadrilateral with two pairs of adjacent sides whose lengths are equal.

- Adjacent sides (the sides next to each other) are the same length
- Diagonals (the lines in the figure above that intersect) cross at right angles

Trapezoids

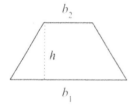

On the ISEE, a *trapezoid* is a quadrilateral with only one pair of parallel sides.

- The sides that are parallel are called *bases*
- The other sides are called *legs*

*The Primary 4 ISEE may use the term *diamond*. This is not a formal mathematical term and does not have a precise definition. You can think of a diamond as a square that has been rotated 45 degrees.

Practice Problems

1. What is the name of a quadrilateral with two pairs of adjacent sides of equal length and no right angles?
    (A)   rectangle
    (B)   trapezoid
    (C)   kite
    (D)   pentagon

2. What is the name of the quadrilateral below?

    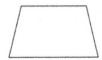

    (A)   parallelogram
    (B)   diamond
    (C)   square
    (D)   trapezoid

3. What is the name of a quadrilateral with sides that measure 4 inches each and four 90-degree angles?
    (A)   octagon
    (B)   square
    (C)   triangle
    (D)   trapezoid

4. What is the name of the quadrilateral below?

    (A)   parallelogram
    (B)   trapezoid
    (C)   rhombus
    (D)   kite

5. How many pairs of parallel sides does a parallelogram have?
    (A)   1
    (B)   2
    (C)   3
    (D)   4

6. Which shapes *always* have four sides of equal length?
    (A)   a rectangle and a trapezoid
    (B)   a parallelogram and a trapezoid
    (C)   a square and a rhombus
    (D)   a kite and a square

7. Which of the following shapes is also always a parallelogram?
    (A)   trapezoid
    (B)   rhombus
    (C)   kite
    (D)   triangle

8. Which of the following shapes is also always a rectangle?
    (A)   square
    (B)   kite
    (C)   parallelogram
    (D)   rhombus

9. Which of the following shapes is also always a quadrilateral?
    (A)   octagon
    (B)   hexagon
    (C)   kite
    (D)   triangle

10. How many degrees are in a right angle?
    (A)   75
    (B)   80
    (C)   85
    (D)   90

11. Is a square always a rectangle?

12. Is a rectangle always a square?

13. Is a square always a rhombus?

14. Is a square always a parallelogram?

15. Is a rhombus always a rectangle?

16. What is the name of a quadrilateral that has one pair of adjacent sides which are 13 inches long, one pair of adjacent sides which are 8 inches long, and diagonals that cross at right angles?

17. A shape has two pairs of parallel sides, its opposite sides are equal, and its opposite angles are equal. What could be the names of the shape?

18. A kite has one side with a length of 5 inches and another side with a length of 8 inches. What is the kite's perimeter?

19. What are parallel lines?

20. What are perpendicular lines?

Clocks and Telling Time

You need to know how to read analog clocks and how to tell time on the Primary 4 ISEE.

There are a few things you must memorize in order to tell time:

1. There are 24 hours in a day

2. There are 60 minutes in 1 hour

3. The short hand on the clock points to the hour

4. The long hand on the clock points to the minute

5. Each number on a clock represents 1 hour. Each number on a clock *also* represents 5 minutes

Telling Time on an Analog Clock

Let's see what this looks like in practice. The clocks below have been divided into sections to make telling time easier. The faces of the clocks have been divided into 12 equally sized sections, each of which has a number inside of it. If the hour hand falls on 6 or anywhere inside the section labeled 6, for example, then the hour is 6. It doesn't matter what part of the section the hour hand lands in.

On the clock above, the short hand is pointing at 8, and the long hand is pointing at 12. That means the hour is 8, and the minutes are 00, so the time is 8:00. On analog clocks, you can't tell if it's A.M. or P.M.

This clock is also divided into 12 sections, but it shows a different time. The hour hand falls into the section labeled 2. The minute hand is pointing at 11. Each number that circles the outside of the clock represents 5 minutes. $11 \times 5 = 55$, so 11 represents 55 minutes. The time on this clock is 2:55.

The hour hand on this clock falls into the 4 section, and the minute hand points to 6. 6 × 5 = 30, so the 6 represents 30 minutes. The time is 4:30.

Finding Elapsed, Starting, and Ending Times
There are 60 minutes in 1 hour. 1 minute after 1:59, for example, is 2:00. It is *not* 1:60! Finding elapsed time is easiest when you work in increments of 1 hour.

Example
It is 1:20 P.M. What time will it be in 2 hours?

In 1 hour, it will be 2:20 P.M. In 2 hours, it will be 3:20 P.M.

Example
It is 3:15 A.M. What time will it be in 3 hours and 10 minutes?

In 3 hours it will be 6:15 A.M. Add on an additional 10 minutes to get 6:25 A.M.

Example
A student started looking for his watch at 4:25 P.M. How much time had elapsed if he found his watch at 6:00 P.M.?

4:25 to 5:25 is 1 hour. 25 to 60 is 35 minutes. 1 hour and 35 minutes had elapsed.

Example
A girl walked her dog for 1 hour and 15 minutes. If she finished walking her dog at 3:25 P.M., what time did she start?

3:25 P.M. minus 1 hour is 2:25 P.M. 2:25 P.M. minus 15 minutes is 2:10 P.M.

Converting Times
To convert minutes to hours, remember that there are 60 minutes in 1 hour.

Example
120 minutes equals how many hours?

120 ÷ 60 = 2. Therefore, 120 minutes equals 2 hours exactly.

Example
186 minutes equals how many hours?

186 ÷ 60 = 3 remainder 6. Therefore, 186 minutes equals 3 hours and 6 minutes.

Practice Problems

Determine the Elapsed Time

1.   2:10 + _____ = 3:10

2.   4:15 + _____ = 7:40

3.   1:35 + _____ = 4:15

4.   10:15 + _____ = 11:55

5.   Joey finished his homework at 6:15 P.M. If he started at 4:00 P.M., how long did it take him to finish?

6.   An infant woke up from a nap at 3:40 P.M. If she originally went to sleep at 1:20 P.M., how long was her nap?

7.   A boy helped his father cook dinner. They finished cooking at 7:05 P.M. If they started cooking at 6:20 P.M., how long did it take them?

8.   Paige went for a bike ride at 5:40 P.M. If she got home at 8:10 P.M., how long was her bike ride?

Determine the Ending Time

9.   2:00 + 3:00 = _____

10.   4:15 + 6:20 = _____

11.   1:25 + 6:30 = _____

12.   11:10 + 0:50 = _____

13. Jessica started jogging at 2:50 P.M. If she jogged for 3 hours and 30 minutes, what time did she finish?

14. Vanessa spent 1 hour and 5 minutes reading a book. If she started reading at 4:05 P.M., what time was it when she finished?

15. Victor went to the movies at 3:30 P.M. If the movie was 2 hours and 40 minutes long, what time was it when Victor finished?

Convert Minutes to Hours

16.   145 minutes equals _____

17.   68 minutes equals _____

18.   230 minutes equals _____

19.   170 minutes equals _____

20.   310 minutes equals _____

Determine the Time Shown

21.

22.

23.

24.

25.

26.

Number Lines

Writing numbers down on a number line makes it easy to tell which numbers are larger and which numbers are smaller.

The number line above demonstrates this concept. The numbers grow larger as you move to the right on the number line. Number lines always go in order from left to right.

On the Primary 4 ISEE, you may be asked questions about number lines with integers or fractions. These questions could test your ability to fill in an empty number line or find equivalent fractions on a number line.

When each tick mark on the number line indicates an increase or decrease of 1, filling in the number line is easy.

Example
Each tick mark on the number line below indicates 1. Fill in the missing tick marks on the number line.

If you know how to add and subtract, you can complete this question without any problems. 1 greater than 17 is 18, so the tick mark to the right of 17 indicates 18. 1 less than 17 is 16, so the tick mark to the left of 17 indicates 16, and so on. You can see the filled in number line below:

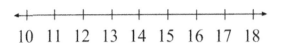

Finding Missing Values on Number Lines

The tick marks on number lines *do not always indicate 1*, and this is where things get more difficult.

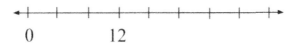

If each tick mark represented 1, then the number line would look like this when you fill it in:

That's obviously incorrect. To determine the value of each tick mark, count the number of equal spaces between 0 and 12. This number line is divided into 3 equally sized sections between 0 and 12.

Find the difference between the labeled points on the number line: $12 - 0 = 12$. Then, divide the difference by the number of equally sized spaces between the two tick marks: $12 \div 3 = 4$. Each tick mark on this number line represents an increase of 4.

This method works regardless of what the two given numbers on the number line are.

Example

Find the value of the tick mark labeled x.

There are 4 equally sized spaces between 6 and 38. $38 - 6 = 32$. $32 \div 4 = 8$. Therefore, each tick mark represents an increase of 8. The completed number line would look like this:

$x = 46$.

Fractions and Number Lines

Finding fractions on number lines works exactly the same way as finding integers.

Example

On the number line below, find the value of each tick mark and fill in the missing tick marks.

There are 6 equally sized spaces between 0 and 1. $1 - 0 = 1$. $1 \div 6 = \frac{1}{6}$. Each tick mark represents an increase of $\frac{1}{6}$

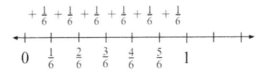

Example

Find the values of x, y, and z on the number line below.

There are 3 equally sized spaces between 1 and 2. $2 - 1 = 1$. $1 \div 3 = \frac{1}{3}$. Each tick mark represents a increase of $\frac{1}{3}$

The value of x is $\frac{2}{3}$, the value of y is $1\frac{1}{3}$, and the value of z is $2\frac{1}{3}$

Equivalent Fractions on Number Lines

You may be asked to find equivalent fractions on number lines.

Example

Using the number lines shown below, what is the equivalent fraction to $\frac{1}{2}$?

On the top number line, there are 2 equally sized spaces between 0 and 1. $1 - 0 = 1$. $1 \div 2 = \frac{1}{2}$. Therefore, each tick mark represents an increase of $\frac{1}{2}$. On the bottom number line, there are 8 equally sized spaces between 0 and 1. $1 - 0 = 1$. $1 \div 8 = \frac{1}{8}$. Therefore, each tick mark represents and increase of $\frac{1}{8}$

The completed number lines will look like this:

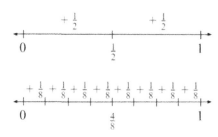

The fraction that is equivalent to $\frac{1}{2}$ is $\frac{4}{8}$

Example

Using the number lines shown below, what is the equivalent fraction to $\frac{4}{6}$?

On the top number line, there are 6 equally sized spaces between 0 and 1. $1 - 0 = 1$. $1 \div 6 = \frac{1}{6}$. Therefore, each tick mark represents an increase of $\frac{1}{6}$. On the bottom number line, there are 3 equally sized spaces between 0 and 1. $1 - 0 = 1$. $1 \div 3 = \frac{1}{3}$. Therefore, each tick mark represents an increase of $\frac{1}{3}$

The completed number lines will look like this:

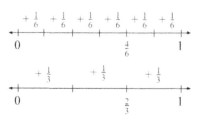

The fraction that is equivalent to $\frac{4}{6}$ is $\frac{2}{3}$

Practice Problems

#1 – 11: find the values of x, y, and z on the number lines.

1.
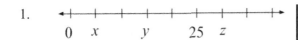

2.
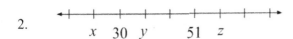

3.
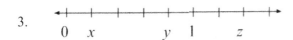

4.
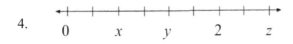

5.

6.
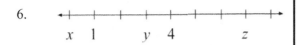

7.
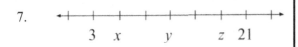

8.

9.

10.
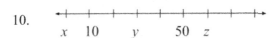

11.

12. On the number line below, what is the equivalent fraction to $\frac{3}{4}$?

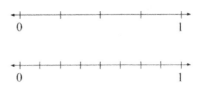

13. On the number line below, what is the equivalent fraction to 1?

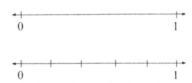

14. On the number line below, what is the equivalent fraction to $\frac{3}{8}$?

Rules of Divisibility

You should memorize the rules of divisibility in the table below. Remember, *divisibility* means one number can be divided by another without leaving a remainder.

A number is divisible by	
2	If the last digit is 0, 2, 4, 6, or 8
3	If the sum of the digits is divisible by 3
5	If the last digit is 0 or 5
9	If the sum of the digits is divisible by 9
10	If the last digit is 0

You may already be familiar with the divisibility rules for 2, 5, and 10. The divisibility rules for 4, 6, 7, and 8 are not included in the table because they are very unlikely to show up on the Primary 4 ISEE.

The divisibility rules for 3 and 9 require a bit more explanation. Take 123 as an example. $1 + 2 + 3 = 6$, and 6 is divisible by 3, which means 123 is divisible by 3. Another example is 999: $9 + 9 + 9 = 27$. 27 is divisible by both 3 and 9, which means 999 is divisible by both 3 and 9.

Memorizing the rules of divisibility will save you a lot of time, since you won't have to spend time actually doing $999 \div 9$ in order to see if there is a remainder.

Practice Problems

1. Which whole number is divisible by 9 without a remainder?
   - (A)   403
   - (B)   405
   - (C)   407
   - (D)   409

2. Which whole number is divisible by 3 without a remainder?
   - (A)   231
   - (B)   233
   - (C)   235
   - (D)   239

3. Which whole number is divisible by 5 without a remainder?
   - (A)   96
   - (B)   98
   - (C)   100
   - (D)   102

4. Which whole number is divisible by 2 without a remainder?
   - (A)   109
   - (B)   111
   - (C)   112
   - (D)   113

5. Which whole number is divisible by 3 without a remainder?
   - (A)   1,372
   - (B)   1,373
   - (C)   1,375
   - (D)   1,377

6. Which whole number is divisible by 5 without a remainder?
   - (A)   15
   - (B)   17
   - (C)   19
   - (D)   21

7. Which whole number is divisible by 9 without a remainder?
   - (A)   939
   - (B)   941
   - (C)   943
   - (D)   945

8. 54 is divisible by which of the following numbers?
   - (A)   3 only
   - (B)   9 only
   - (C)   3 and 9
   - (D)   2, 3, and 9

9. 270 is divisible by which of the following numbers?
   - (A)   3 only
   - (B)   5 only
   - (C)   3, 5, and 9
   - (D)   2, 3, 5, 9, and 10

10. 303 is divisible by which of the following numbers?
    - (A)   3 only
    - (B)   9 only
    - (C)   3 and 9
    - (D)   2, 3, and 9

11. Which whole number is divisible by 10 without a remainder?
    - (A)   1,001
    - (B)   1,010
    - (C)   1,011
    - (D)   1,111

12. 240 is divisible by which of the following numbers?
    - (A)   2 only
    - (B)   2, 3, and 9
    - (C)   2, 3, and 5
    - (D)   2, 3, 5, and 9

Coordinate Grids

On the Primary 4 ISEE, you will be asked to plot points on a coordinate grid. The figure below shows an example of a coordinate grid:

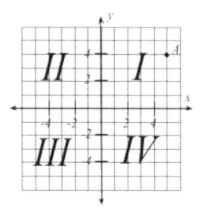

Coordinate grids are divided into four quadrants. The grids are composed of an x-axis, which runs horizontally, and a y-axis, which runs vertically. The axes intersect at the origin. The coordinates of the origin are (0,0).

To find the coordinates of a point on the coordinate plane, start at the origin (the place where the x- and y-axes intersect) and count how far you must move on the x-axis. If you move to the right, the coordinate is positive. If you move to the left, the coordinate is negative. Then, count how far up and down you must move on the y-axis. If you move up, the coordinate is positive. If you move down, the coordinate is negative.

Some students find it helpful to think about coordinates like this: to get to a friend's apartment, first you have to walk to his or her building, then you have to take the elevator up to the apartment. If you walk to the right on the x-axis, the coordinate is positive; if you walk to the left on the x-axis, the coordinate is negative. Then, if you take the elevator up to your friend's apartment, the second coordinate is positive; if you take the elevator down to the basement, the second coordinate is negative.

Point A is labeled in the grid above. Beginning at the origin, move right 5 spaces, then move up 4 spaces. The coordinates of Point A are (5, 4).

Practice Problems

1. What are the coordinates of Point *A* on the graph below?

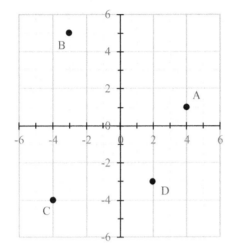

    (A)   (4,-1)
    (B)   (4,1)
    (C)   (3,-1)
    (D)   (5,1)

2. What are the coordinates of Point *B* on the graph below?

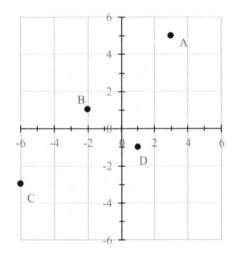

    (A)   (2,1)
    (B)   (2,-1)
    (C)   (-2,-1)
    (D)   (-2,1)

3. What are the coordinates of Point *C* on the graph below?

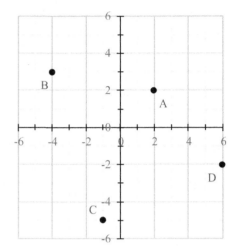

    (A)   (-1,-4)
    (B)   (0,-5)
    (C)   (-1,-5)
    (D)   (-5,-1)

4. What are the coordinates of Point *D* on the graph below?

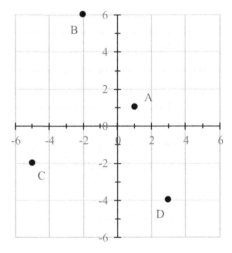

    (A)   (3,3)
    (B)   (-4,3)
    (C)   (3,4)
    (D)   (3,-4)

5. What are the coordinates of Point *E* on the graph below?

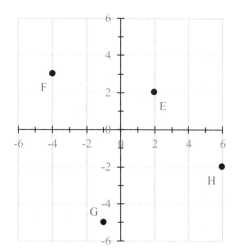

(A)   (-2,-2)

(B)   (2,2)

(C)   (1,1)

(D)   (-4,3)

6. What are the coordinates of Point *F* on the graph below?

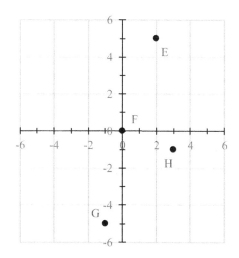

(A)   (0,0)

(B)   (1,1)

(C)   (-1,-1)

(D)   (0,1)

7. What are the coordinates of Point *G* on the graph below?

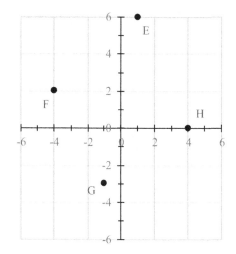

(A)   (-3,-1)

(B)   (-1,-2)

(C)   (-1,-3)

(D)   (0,-3)

8. What are the coordinates of Point *H* on the graph below?

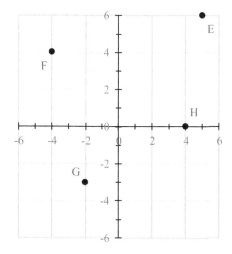

(A)   (4,0)

(B)   (0,4)

(C)   (-4,0)

(D)   (0,-4)

Currency

On the Primary 4 ISEE, you will need to be comfortable identifying coins, knowing the value of coins, and performing operations such as adding and subtracting coins.

There are four coins you should be familiar with:

Penny	Dime	Nickel	Quarter
1 cent	10 cents	5 cents	25 cents
$0.01	$0.10	$0.05	$0.25

There are 100 cents in 1 dollar. 1 dollar is also written as *$1.00*. 100 pennies added together equal 1 dollar, 10 dimes added together equal 1 dollar, 20 nickels added together equal 1 dollar, and 4 quarters added together equal 1 dollar.

There are two ways of adding and subtracting money. First, you can think of everything in cents. For example, 1 dollar + 1 quarter + 1 dime = 100 cents + 25 cents + 10 cents = 135.00 cents. Then, move the decimal two places to the left to get $1.35

Or, you can think of it this way: 1 dollar + 1 quarter + 1 dime = $1.00 + $0.25 + $0.10 = $1.35

Example
How many pennies are in 5 quarters?

1 quarter = 25 cents, so 5 quarters = 125 cents. 1 penny = 1 cent. 125 ÷ 1 = 125. There are 125 pennies in 5 quarters.

Example
How many dimes are in 16 nickels?

1 nickel = 5 cents, so 16 nickels = 80 cents. 1 dime = 10 cents. 80 ÷ 10 = 8. There are 8 dimes in 16 nickels.

Example
A student has 9 pennies, 4 nickels, 4 dimes, and 2 quarters. How much money does the student have?

9 pennies = 9 cents. 4 nickels = 20 cents. 4 dimes = 40 cents. 2 quarters = 50 cents.

9 + 20 + 40 + 50 = 119 cents or $1.19.

Practice Problems

1. Identify the coin below:

2. Identify the coin below:

3. Identify the coin below:

4. Identify the coin below:

5. How many pennies are in 1 dollar?

6. How many nickels are in 1 dollar?

7. How many dimes are in 1 dollar?

8. How many quarters are in 1 dollar?

9. How many pennies are in 3 quarters?

10. How many dimes are in 2 quarters?

11. How many nickels are in 6 dimes?

12. How many quarters are in 4 dollars?

13. A student has 2 pennies, 3 nickels, and 4 dimes. How much money does the student have?

14. A student has 8 pennies, 2 nickels, 3 dimes, and 1 quarter. How much money does the student have?

15. A student has 12 nickels, 4 dimes, and 2 quarters. How much money does the student have?

16. A student has 22 pennies, 5 nickels, 3 dimes, and 1 quarter. How much money does the student have?

17. A student has 45 pennies, 2 nickels, and 2 dimes. How much money does the student have?

18. A student has 100 pennies, 14 nickels, and 1 quarter. How much money does the student have?

19. A student has 32 pennies, 5 nickels, 2 dimes, and 2 quarters. How much money does the student have?

20. A student has 14 pennies, 20 nickels, 4 dimes, and 7 quarters. How much money does the student have?

Probability

Probability tells you the likelihood of something happening. It is expressed as a number between 0 (event never occurs) and 1 (event always occurs). Probability can be expressed as a fraction, decimal, or percent.

$$\text{Probability} = \frac{number\ of\ favorable\ outcomes}{total\ possible\ number\ of\ outcomes}$$

Example

What is the probability of flipping heads on a coin?

This one is easy. There are two possible outcomes: heads or tails. Heads is a "favorable outcome," so it goes in the numerator. The probability of flipping heads is $\frac{1}{2}$

Example

What is the probability of rolling a 3 or a 4 on a die?

Another easy one! There are six possible outcomes, and two of them are "favorable." The probability of rolling a 3 or a 4 on a die is $\frac{2}{6} = \frac{1}{3}$

Example

A boy has a box of crayons, all of which are either red or yellow. He wants to use a red crayon to draw a picture. There are 6 yellow crayons and 4 red crayons in the box. If the boy pulls crayons from the box without looking, how many crayons does he need to pull out to ensure that at least one of the crayons is red?

(A)   4
(B)   5
(C)   7
(D)   8

This question is somewhat confusing, but it's not actually very difficult. If the question asked what the *probability* of pulling out a red crayon on the first try is, the answer would be $\frac{4}{10} = \frac{2}{5}$, because there are 4 red crayons and 10 crayons in total. However, that's not what the question is asking. This question asks how many crayons must be pulled out to *guarantee* that one of the crayons pulled out is red. The only way to *guarantee* that the boy pulls out a red crayon is if he has pulled out every yellow crayon first, so that only red crayons remain. So, he would pull out 6 yellow crayons, and on the 7th attempt, he would pull out a red crayon. **The correct answer is (C).**

Keep in mind that it is unlikely that is would take 7 attempts to pull out a red crayon. The order of crayons could be Y, Y, R, Y, R, Y, Y, Y, R, R or R, Y, R, R, Y, Y, Y, Y, R, Y, etc. But, it is *possible* that the order of crayons is Y, Y, Y, Y, Y, Y, R, R, R, R, and that is why it is necessary to pull out 7 crayons to *guarantee* that the 7th crayon will be red.

Example

A student has a bag full of 24 colored blocks, entirely consisting of red blocks, blue blocks, and green blocks. If half the blocks are red and a third of the blocks are blue, what is the probability of randomly selecting a green block from the bag?

(A)   1 out of 3
(B)   1 out of 4
(C)   1 out of 6
(D)   1 out of 8

This is a difficult question that tests your knowledge of probability and fractions. Unless you feel very comfortable with both these topics, we recommend you guess on a question like this on the test. First, figure out how many blocks are red. This isn't too difficult: half of 24 is 12, so 12 blocks are red. Finding how many blocks are blue is slightly harder. If you know how to multiply fractions, you can do $\frac{1}{3} \times 24 = 8$. Therefore, 4 of the blocks are green, because $24 - 12 - 8 = 4$. 4 out of 24 blocks are green. Divide both these numbers by 4 to get 1 out of 6. **The correct answer is (C).**

Practice Problems

1. A man has a drawer of 2 black and 6 white shirts. He knows that he wants to wear a white shirt today. If he pulls out his shirts without looking, how many shirts does he need to pull out to make sure that at least one of the shirts is white?
    (A)   1
    (B)   2
    (C)   3
    (D)   4

2. What is the probability of rolling a 3 on a 6-sided die?

    (A) $\frac{1}{2}$

    (B) $\frac{1}{3}$

    (C) $\frac{1}{5}$

    (D) $\frac{1}{6}$

3. A bag holds 3 red marbles, 2 blue marbles, and 4 yellow marbles. If a marble is selected at random, what is the probability it will be yellow?

    (A) $\frac{4}{7}$

    (B) $\frac{4}{5}$

    (C) $\frac{4}{9}$

    (D)   4

4. A student has a bag full of 48 colored blocks, entirely consisting of orange blocks, black blocks, and yellow blocks. If a quarter of the blocks are orange and a third of the blocks are black, what is the probability of randomly selecting a yellow block from the bag?
    (A)   5 out of 12
    (B)   1 out of 2
    (C)   3 out of 8
    (D)   1 out of 4

5. A bag holds 2 red marbles, 5 blue marbles, and 6 yellow marbles. If a marble is selected at random, what is the probability it will be red or blue?

    (A) $\dfrac{7}{13}$

    (B) $\dfrac{2}{13}$

    (C) $\dfrac{7}{6}$

    (D) $\dfrac{5}{13}$

6. In a drawer, there are 16 pieces of silverware, entirely consisting of forks, knives, and spoons. If half are spoons and a quarter are forks, what is the probability of randomly selecting a knife from the drawer?
    (A)   1 out of 2
    (B)   1 out of 3
    (C)   1 out of 4
    (D)   1 out of 5

7. A student has a box that contains 5 green pens and 6 black pens. If the student pulls pens out of the box without looking, how many pens will the student have to pull out to make sure that she pulls out a black pen?
    (A)   1
    (B)   3
    (C)   6
    (D)   7

8. What is the probability of rolling an even number on a 6-sided die?

    (A) $\dfrac{1}{6}$

    (B) $\dfrac{1}{2}$

    (C) $\dfrac{1}{3}$

    (D) $\dfrac{1}{4}$

9. There are 10 boys and 15 girls in a class. If a teacher selects a student at random, what is the probability that the student will be a girl?

    (A) $\dfrac{5}{3}$

    (B) $\dfrac{15}{20}$

    (C) $\dfrac{15}{10}$

    (D) $\dfrac{3}{5}$

10. A student has a box that contains 4 yellow markers and 9 blue markers. If the student pulls markers out of the box without looking, how many markers will the student have to pull out to make sure that he pulls out a yellow marker?
    (A)   9
    (B)   10
    (C)   11
    (D)   12

11. A student has a set of 32 crayons, entirely consisting of pink crayons, purple crayons, and brown crayons. If a quarter of the crayons are pink and half of the crayons are purple, what is the probability of randomly selecting a brown crayon?
    (A)   1 out of 10
    (B)   1 out of 8
    (C)   1 out of 6
    (D)   1 out of 4

12. There are 7 girls and 8 boys in a class. If a teacher selects a student at random, what is the probability that the student will be a boy?

    (A) $\frac{8}{15}$

    (B) $\frac{8}{7}$

    (C) $\frac{7}{8}$

    (D) $\frac{7}{15}$

13. A man has a drawer filled with 3 red shirts, 7 blue shirts, 2 black shirts, and 4 red shirts. If he selects a shirt without looking, what is the probability that shirt will be either blue or black?

    (A) $\frac{16}{9}$

    (B) $\frac{7}{9}$

    (C) $\frac{9}{7}$

    (D) $\frac{9}{16}$

14. A student has a bag full of 100 colored blocks, entirely consisting of magenta blocks, vermillion blocks, and ochre blocks. If a tenth of the blocks are magenta and half of the blocks are vermillion, what is the probability of randomly selecting an ochre block from the bag?
    (A)   1 out of 5
    (B)   2 out of 5
    (C)   3 out of 5
    (D)   4 out of 5

15. What is the probability of rolling any number but 6 on a 6-sided die?

    (A) $\frac{1}{6}$

    (B) $\frac{5}{6}$

    (C) $\frac{2}{3}$

    (D) $\frac{1}{3}$

16. A woman has a drawer of 3 blue shirts, 4 black shirts, and 7 red shirts. She knows that she wants to wear a red shirt today. If she pulls out her shirts without looking, how many shirts does she need to pull out to make sure that at least one of the shirts is red?
    (A)   8
    (B)   9
    (C)   10
    (D)   11

17. A student has a bag of 64 marbles, entirely consisting of blue marbles, white marbles, and yellow marbles. If an eighth of the marbles are blue and a quarter of the marbles are white, what is the probability of randomly selecting a yellow marble?
    (A)   3 out of 8
    (B)   4 out of 8
    (C)   5 out of 8
    (D)   6 out of 8

Answer Key – Mathematics Fundamentals

Math Definitions

1. Possible answers include -50, -8, 0, 1, 2, 34, etc
2. Possible answers include 2, 3, 5, 7, 11, 13, 17, 19, etc
3. No
4. Yes
5. Possible answers include 1, 2, 3, 4, or -11, -10, -9, -8, etc
6. 20
7. Possible answers include 4, 8, 12, 16, 20, 24, etc
8. 6
9. 10
10. 15
11. Possible answers include 4, 6, 8, 9, 10, 12, 14, 15, 16, etc
12. 40
13. 34
14. 1, 2, 4, 8, and 16
15. Possible answers include 3, 6, 9, 12, 15, 18, 21, etc
16. Even
17. No
18. 38
19. No
20. Yes

PEMDAS

1. 18
2. 22
3. 8
4. 17
5. 12
6. 4
7. 1
8. 10
9. 36
10. 7

Reducing Fractions

Reduce

1. $\frac{1}{2}$
2. $\frac{3}{5}$
3. $\frac{1}{3}$
4. $\frac{1}{1}$ or 1
5. $\frac{58}{111}$
6. $\frac{5}{9}$
7. $\frac{1}{3}$
8. $\frac{63}{47}$
9. $\frac{4}{3}$
10. $\frac{2}{1}$ or 2
11. $\frac{16}{17}$
12. $\frac{1}{5}$
13. $\frac{1}{10}$
14. $\frac{1}{3}$
15. $\frac{1}{2}$
16. $\frac{1}{8}$
17. $\frac{1}{3}$
18. $\frac{4}{5}$
19. $\frac{2}{5}$
20. $\frac{2}{3}$

Improper Fractions and Mixed Numbers

Convert to Mixed Numbers

1. $2\frac{1}{4}$

2. $2\frac{2}{5}$

3. $1\frac{19}{80}$

4. $1\frac{10}{40}$ or $1\frac{1}{4}$

5. $6\frac{3}{4}$

6. $1\frac{1}{16}$

7. $1\frac{1}{2}$

8. $1\frac{43}{45}$

Convert to Improper Fractions

9. $\frac{9}{7}$

10. $\frac{11}{4}$

11. $\frac{17}{12}$

12. $\frac{35}{8}$

13. $\frac{31}{9}$

14. $\frac{26}{5}$

15. $\frac{14}{3}$

16. $\frac{80}{9}$

Convert to Whole Numbers

17. 2
18. 10
19. 4
20. 1
21. 3

Operations with Fractions

Add, Subtract, Multiply, or Divide

1. $\frac{7}{9}$

2. $\frac{45}{44}$ or $1\frac{1}{44}$

3. $\frac{18}{49}$

4. $\frac{2}{12}$ or $\frac{1}{6}$

5. $\frac{57}{40}$ or $1\frac{17}{40}$

6. $\frac{28}{25}$ or $1\frac{3}{25}$

7. $\frac{4}{13}$

8. $\frac{3}{8}$

9. $\frac{36}{33}$ or $\frac{12}{11}$ or $1\frac{1}{11}$

10. $\frac{6}{63}$ or $\frac{2}{21}$

Which Fraction is Larger?

11. $\frac{3}{8}$

12. $\frac{3}{4}$

13. $\frac{1}{6}$

14. The fractions are equal

15. $\frac{6}{8}$

Solve

16. B
17. A
18. C
19. A
20. D
21. C
22. C

Decimals

1.   2.044
2.   3.3302
3.   5.509
4.   18.84
5.   0.292
6.   10.94
7.   10.202
8.   0.7274

9. $\frac{55}{100}$ or $\frac{11}{20}$

10   $\frac{9}{100}$

11. $\frac{40}{100}$ or $\frac{2}{5}$

12. $\frac{12}{100}$ or $\frac{3}{25}$

13. $\frac{95}{100}$ or $\frac{19}{20}$

14.   0.43
15.   0.06
16.   0.93
17.   0.01
18.   0.55

Percents

Convert Fractions to Percents

1.   14%
2.   65%
3.   50%
4.   90%
5.   80%
6.   75%

Convert the Percents to Decimals

7.   0.90
8.   0.65
9.   0.03
10.   0.12

Convert the Percents to Fractions

11. $\frac{15}{100}$ or $\frac{3}{20}$

12. $\frac{28}{100}$ or $\frac{7}{25}$

13. $\frac{63}{100}$

14. $\frac{44}{100}$ or $\frac{11}{25}$

Units of Measurement

1.   Inches, centimeters
2.   Grams, kilograms, pounds
3.   Ounces, milliliters
4.   Liters, gallons
5.   Pounds, kilograms
6.   Feet, meters
7.   Pounds, kilograms
8.   Inches, centimeters

Perimeter and Area

1.   36 square centimeters
2.   20 inches
3.   48 square feet
4.   20 centimeters
5.   20 feet
6.   24 square centimeters
7.   30 meters
8.   60 inches
9.   9 inches
10.   9 feet
11.   20 centimeters
12.   28 centimeters
13.   18 square feet
14.   Perimeter
15.   36 inches

Mathematical Properties

1.   Identity
2.   Commutative
3.   Identity
4.   Associative
5.   Distributive
6.   Identity
7.   Associative
8.   Commutative
9.   Distributive
10. Commutative

Shapes

1.   9
2.   Hexagon
3.   13
4.   8
5.   Heptagons
6.   Decagon
7.   17
8.   Heptagon
9.   5 centimeters
10. 8 inches
11. 49 inches
12. 27 meters
13. 12 centimeters
14. 42 inches
15. 15
16. 60 inches
17. 10
18. Hexagon
19. Triangle, Quadrilateral, Pentagon, Hexagon, Heptagon, Octagon, Nonagon, Decagon
20. All the shape's sides are equal and all of the shape's interior angles are equal
21. 19

Quadrilaterals

1.   C
2.   D
3.   B
4.   A
5.   B
6.   C
7.   B
8.   A
9.   C
10. D
11. Yes
12. No
13. Yes
14. Yes
15. No
16. Kite
17. Square, Rectangle, Parallelogram, Rhombus, or Kite
18. 26 inches
19. A pair of lines that have the same distance continuously between them and never intersect
20. Two lines that intersect at 90-degree angles

Clocks and Telling Time

Determine the Elapsed Time

1.   1 hour
2.   3 hours 25 minutes
3.   2 hours 40 minutes
4.   1 hour 40 minutes
5.   2 hours 15 minutes
6.   2 hours 20 minutes
7.   45 minutes
8.   2 hours 30 minutes

Determine the Ending Time

9.   5:00
10.   10:35
11.   7:55
12.   12:00
13.   6:20 P.M.
14.   5:10 P.M.
15.   6:10 P.M.

Convert Minutes to Hours

16.   2 hours 25 minutes
17.   1 hour 8 minutes
18.   3 hours 50 minutes
19.   2 hours 50 minutes
20.   5 hours 10 minutes

Determine the Time Shown

21.   3:35
22.   11:55
23.   9:40
24.   10:10
25.   9:20
26.   12:20

Number Lines

1. $x = 5, y = 15, z = 30$

2. $x = 23, y = 37, z = 58$

3. $x = \frac{1}{5}, y = \frac{4}{5}, z = \frac{7}{5}$ or $1\frac{2}{5}$

4. $x = \frac{2}{3}, y = \frac{4}{3}$ or $1\frac{1}{3}, z = \frac{8}{3}$ or $2\frac{2}{3}$

5. $x = 12, y = 24, z = 28$

6. $x = 0, y = 3, z = 7$

7. $x = 6, y = 12, z = 18$

8. $x = 12, y = 30, z = 42$

9. $x = 36, y = 60, z = 96$

10. $x = 0, y = 30, z = 60$

11. $x = 15, y = 30, z = 40$

12. $\frac{6}{8}$

13. $\frac{5}{5}$

14. $\frac{6}{16}$

Rules of Divisibility

1.   B
2.   A
3.   C
4.   C
5.   D
6.   A
7.   D
8.   D
9.   D
10.   A
11.   B
12.   C

Coordinate Grids

1. B
2. D
3. C
4. D
5. B
6. A
7. C
8. A

Currency

1. Quarter
2. Nickel
3. Penny
4. Dime
5. 100
6. 20
7. 10
8. 4
9. 75
10. 5
11. 12
12. 16
13. 57 cents or $0.57
14. 73 cents or $0.73
15. 150 cents or $1.50
16. 102 cents or $1.02
17. 75 cents or $0.75
18. 195 cents or $1.95
19. 127 cents or $1.27
20. 329 cents or $3.29

Probability

1. C
2. D
3. C
4. A
5. A
6. C
7. C
8. B
9. D
10. B
11. D
12. A
13. D
14. B
15. B
16. A
17. C

Part IV
Mathematics Question Types

Graphs

Graphs require that you understand large amounts of information. When you see a graph question, the first thing you should do is look at the *x*- and *y*- axes. The *x*-axis is horizontal (it goes left to right); it will be labeled on the bottom part of the graph. The *y*-axis is vertical (it goes up and down); it will be labeled on the left or right side of the graph. There may also be a *key* which provides some additional information. Once you have a general idea of what is going on in the graph, look at the related question so you know where you should focus your attention.

Example #1
Questions #1 – 4 refer to the graph below.

A teacher created a graph to compare the favorite pets of the students in her class.

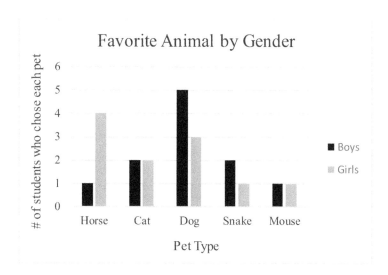

1. Which animal did more girls prefer than boys?
    (A)   Horse
    (B)   Cat
    (C)   Dog
    (D)   Snake

2. How many boys liked either cats or dogs?
    (A)   3
    (B)   4
    (C)   7
    (D)   8

3. Which animal was preferred by the greatest total number of students?
    (A)   Cat
    (B)   Dog
    (C)   Snake
    (D)   Mouse

4. How many more boys than girls preferred snakes?
    (A)   1
    (B)   2
    (C)   3
    (D)   4

On this graph, the *x*-axis shows which animal students preferred, while the *y*-axis indicates how many students preferred each animal. There is also a key to the side of the graph that tells you the boys' responses are labeled in black, while the girls' responses are labeled in grey.

Now that you understand what's going on in the graph, answering the questions will be easy. For question 1, you can see that the only animal on the graph that has a taller bar for girls than boys is horses, **so the correct answer is (A)**. Question 2 requires that you do a little addition. 2 boys liked cats and 5 boys liked dogs, so 7 boys liked either cats or dogs. **The correct answer is (C).** 8 total students preferred dogs, so **the correct answer for question 3 is (B).** Finally, you can see that 2 boys and 1 girl preferred snakes, and 2 − 1 = 1, so **the correct answer for question 4 is (A).**

Practice Problems

Questions #1 – 4 refer to the graph below.

A teacher created a graph to record what types of pets the students in his class own.

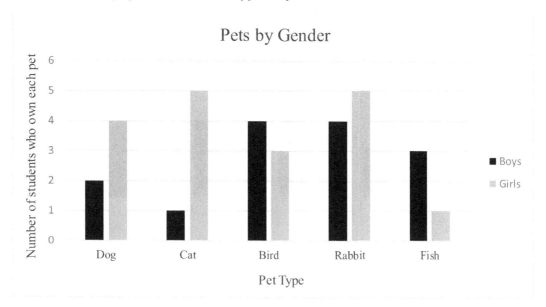

1. Which pet had the greatest difference between the number of boys and the number of girls who owned that pet?
   (A)   Dog
   (B)   Cat
   (C)   Bird
   (D)   Fish

2. How many boys owned either a bird or a fish?
   (A)   3
   (B)   4
   (C)   7
   (D)   8

3. Which type of animal had the greatest total number of boys and girls who owned that pet?
   (A)   Cat
   (B)   Rabbit
   (C)   Fish
   (D)   Dog

4. How many more boys than girls owned a fish?
   (A)   1
   (B)   2
   (C)   3
   (D)   4

Questions #5 – 10 refer to the graph below.

Students in a class voted for their favorite movie.

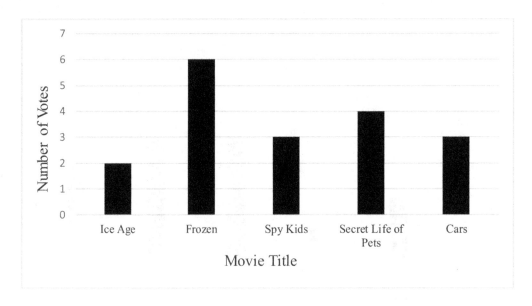

5. How many students voted for *Spy Kids*?
    (A)   1
    (B)   2
    (C)   3
    (D)   4

6. Which movie received the most votes?
    (A)   *Ice Age*
    (B)   *Spy Kids*
    (C)   *Cars*
    (D)   *Frozen*

7. Which two movies received the same number of votes?
    (A)   *Ice Age* and *Spy Kids*
    (B)   *Spy Kids* and *Cars*
    (C)   *Frozen* and *Secret Life of Pets*
    (D)   *Ice Age* and *Frozen*

8. Which movie received 4 votes?
    (A)   *Frozen*
    (B)   *Spy Kids*
    (C)   *Secret Life of Pets*
    (D)   *Cars*

9. How many more votes did *Spy Kids* receive than *Ice Age*?
    (A)   1
    (B)   2
    (C)   3
    (D)   4

10. What is the combined number of students who voted for *Cars* and *Spy Kids*?
    (A)   3
    (B)   4
    (C)   5
    (D)   6

Questions #11 – 14 refer to the graph below.

The graph represents the number of boys and girls in all the classes in each grade at an elementary school.

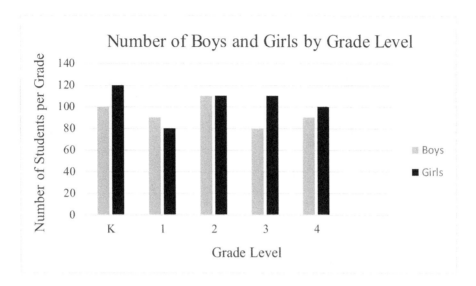

11. Based on the data in this graph, which question can be answered?
    (A)   Which grade has the most classrooms?
    (B)   How many boys and girls are in 5th grade?
    (C)   Which grade has the greatest number of students?
    (D)   How many boys and girls will be in kindergarten next year?

12. How many more boys are there in kindergarten than there are in 3rd grade?
    (A)   1
    (B)   2
    (C)   10
    (D)   20

13. Which grade has fewer girls than boys?
    (A)   Kindergarten
    (B)   1st
    (C)   2nd
    (D)   3rd

14. Which grade has the same number of boys and girls?
    (A)   1st
    (B)   2nd
    (C)   3rd
    (D)   4th

15. Determine which graph best represents the information in the table.

Student Name	Faye	Pierre	Hannah	Anik	Kelly
States Lived In	2	3	7	2	7

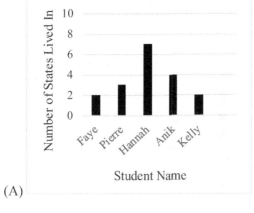

(A)

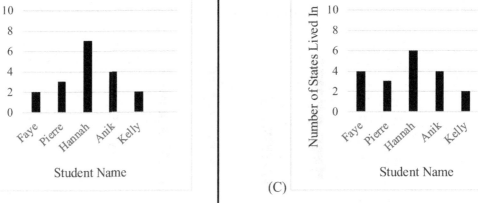

(C)

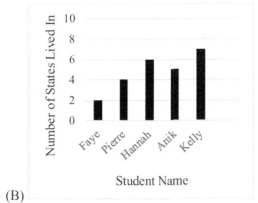

(B)

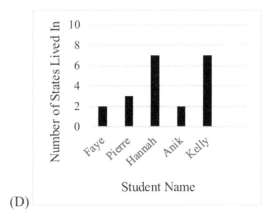

(D)

Tables

Tables questions usually test your ability to identify trends with decimals or rates.

Example #1
Mehmet recorded how much time he spent doing dishes for 10 consecutive days.

DISHWASHING TIMES FOR NOVEMBER 3-12	
Nov 3	7.55 minutes
Nov 4	7.78 minutes
Nov 5	7.91 minutes
Nov 6	8.01 minutes
Nov 7	8.19 minutes
Nov 8	8.47 minutes
Nov 9	8.41 minutes
Nov 10	8.65 minutes
Nov 11	9.00 minutes
Nov 12	9.05 minutes

The amount of time Mehmet spent washing dishes each day increased for several days, then decreased. On which day did the amount of time Mehmet spent washing dishes decrease?

(A)   Nov 7
(B)   Nov 8
(C)   Nov 9
(D)   Nov 10

There is a lot of information in this table. Put your finger next to the "minutes" column on the right and slowly trace from top to bottom. As you go, pay very close attention to the times. At first, the times only increase, going from 7.55 minutes on November 3rd to 8.47 minutes on November 8th. On November 9th, the time drops to 8.41 minutes. Therefore, **(C) is the correct answer**. You don't even need to bother looking at (D)!

Example #2
The table shows the number of copies made per minute with a school's new copy machine.

NEW COPY MACHINE	
Number of Copies	Minutes
60	5
120	6
180	7

Jenny needs to make 360 copies. How long will it take Jenny to make 360 copies?

(A)   9 minutes
(B)   10 minutes
(C)   11 minutes
(D)   12 minutes

It takes 5 minutes to make the first 60 copies and 1 minute to make 60 copies after that. Jenny needs to make 180 + 60 + 60 + 60 = 360 copies. This will take 7 + 1 + 1 + 1 = 10 minutes. **The correct answer is (B).**

Example #3

The following table displays information about class pets.

Pet	# of students
Dog	7
Cat	1
Fish	4
Bird	3

How many students owned either a dog or a bird, assuming none owned both?

(A)   3
(B)   7
(C)   10
(D)   13

This is a very easy question! All you have to do is see how many students own a dog and how many students own a bird, and then find the sum. 7 students own a dog and 3 students own a bird. $7 + 3 = 10$. **(C) is the correct answer.**

Example #4

The table below shows the results of 6 exams for two students.

Exam	Student 1	Student 2
1	Pass	Fail
2	Pass	Fail
3	Fail	Pass
4	Pass	Pass
5	Fail	Fail
6	Pass	Fail

What is the difference in the number of tests passed by each of the two students?
(A)   1
(B)   2
(C)   3
(D)   4

This is not a difficult question; you just need to know that *difference* is the result of subtraction. You should review the terms from Math Definitions in Part III to make sure you know the meaning of sum, difference, product, and quotient. Student 1 passed 4 tests, while student 2 passed 2 tests. $4 - 2 = 2$. **The correct answer is (B).**

Practice Problems

1. Alban recorded how long it took him to run a mile for 9 consecutive days.

MILE TIMES FOR JUNE 20-28	
June 20	9.25 minutes
June 21	9.17 minutes
June 22	9.05 minutes
June 23	8.55 minutes
June 24	8.37 minutes
June 25	7.59 minutes
June 26	7.51 minutes
June 27	7.55 minutes
June 28	7.45 minutes

Alban's times decreased each day for several days and then increased. On which day did his time increase?
(A) June 23
(B) June 25
(C) June 27
(D) June 28

2. The following table displays information about class pets.

Pet	# of students
Rabbit	3
Snake	2
Dog	6
Mouse	3
Parakeet	8

How many students owned either a snake or a parakeet, assuming none owned both?
(A) 2
(B) 4
(C) 8
(D) 10

3. The table shows the number of copies made per minute with the school's new copy machine.

NEW COPY MACHINE	
Number of Copies	Minutes
60	5
120	6
180	7
240	8

Aria needs to make 420 copies. How long will it take Aria to make 420 copies?
(A) 11 minutes
(B) 12 minutes
(C) 13 minutes
(D) 14 minutes

4. The table below shows the results of 8 exams for two students.

Exam	Student 1	Student 2
1	Pass	Pass
2	Fail	Pass
3	Fail	Pass
4	Fail	Pass
5	Pass	Pass
6	Fail	Fail
7	Pass	Fail
8	Pass	Fail

What is the product of the number of exams failed by the two students?
(A) 1
(B) 7
(C) 12
(D) 20

5. A coach recorded a swimmer's swim times for 10 consecutive days.

SWIM TIMES FOR APRIL 10-19	
April 10	32.4 seconds
April 11	31.8 seconds
April 12	31.6 seconds
April 13	31.4 seconds
April 14	31.2 seconds
April 15	31.6 seconds
April 16	30.8 seconds
April 17	30.6 seconds
April 18	30.4 seconds
April 19	29.8 seconds

The swimmer's times decreased each day for several days and then increased. On which day did the time increase?
(A)   April 13
(B)   April 14
(C)   April 15
(D)   April 16

6. Two friends, Samantha and Diane, competed to see who could collect the most pieces of trash on the beach. Here are the results over 5 days:

Day	Samantha	Diane
1	26	27
2	20	22
3	18	31
4	25	19
5	33	25

How many total pieces of trash were collected by the girl who won the competition?
(A)   121
(B)   122
(C)   123
(D)   124

7. The table below shows how many baskets two students made during 7 rounds of basketball.

Round	Student 1	Student 2
1	2	5
2	4	5
3	1	2
4	7	4
5	4	8
6	3	3
7	6	1

What is the difference in the total number of baskets made by each of the two students?
(A)   0
(B)   1
(C)   45
(D)   55

8. Two schools, Fieldston and Poly Prep, competed on the number of community service projects their respective students could organize. Here are the results over 5 years:

Year	Fieldston	Poly Prep
1	22	14
2	15	24
3	18	15
4	13	15
5	12	17

How many total projects were completed by the school that lost the competition?
(A)   75
(B)   80
(C)   85
(D)   90

9. Yosef recorded how long it took him to complete his homework each day for 10 consecutive days.

HOMEWORK TIME FOR JANUARY 12-21	
Jan 12	46.20 minutes
Jan 13	45.90 minutes
Jan 14	43.10 minutes
Jan 15	43.05 minutes
Jan 16	43.50 minutes
Jan 17	43.60 minutes
Jan 18	43.65 minutes
Jan 19	44.10 minutes
Jan 20	44.25 minutes
Jan 21	44.90 minutes

Yosef's homework completion time decreased for several days before beginning to increase again. On which day did his time begin to increase?
(A)   Jan 15
(B)   Jan 16
(C)   Jan 17
(D)   Jan 18

10. The table shows how far Mateo walks in a certain amount of time.

Distance Walked (miles)	Minutes
0.50	10
1.00	20
1.50	30
2.00	40

At his current rate, how far will Mateo walk in 100 minutes?
(A)   2.50 miles
(B)   4.00 miles
(C)   5.00 miles
(D)   6.50 miles

11. The following table displays information about students' favorite colors.

Color	# of students
Red	7
Blue	9
Yellow	4
Green	8
Pink	6

How many students preferred red or pink, assuming none liked both?
(A)   6
(B)   7
(C)   12
(D)   13

12. The table below shows the results of 9 exams for two students.

Exam	Student 1	Student 2
1	Pass	Pass
2	Fail	Pass
3	Pass	Pass
4	Fail	Pass
5	Fail	Pass
6	Fail	Fail
7	Pass	Fail
8	Pass	Pass
9	Pass	Fail

What is the difference in the number of tests passed by each of the two students?
(A)   1
(B)   2
(C)   3
(D)   4

13. Aya recorded how much time she spent watching TV each day for 10 consecutive days.

TV TIME FOR DECEMBER 15-24	
Dec 15	36.40 minutes
Dec 16	33.15 minutes
Dec 17	30.50 minutes
Dec 18	36.75 minutes
Dec 19	37.15 minutes
Dec 20	36.65 minutes
Dec 21	31.45 minutes
Dec 22	32.50 minutes
Dec 23	33.00 minutes
Dec 24	29.25 minutes

On which day did Aya watch 0.50 fewer minutes of TV than she did the day before?

(A)   Dec 16
(B)   Dec 19
(C)   Dec 20
(D)   Dec 22

14. The table below shows the results of 6 exams for two students.

Exam	Student 1	Student 2
1	Pass	Pass
2	Fail	Pass
3	Pass	Pass
4	Fail	Pass
5	Fail	Pass
6	Fail	Fail

What is the difference in the number of tests passed by each of the two students?

(A)   2
(B)   3
(C)   4
(D)   5

15. The table shows the distance Liam swims in a certain amount of time.

Distance (meters)	Seconds
30	20
50	40
70	60
90	80

At his current rate, how many seconds will it take for Liam to swim 120 meters?

(A)   100
(B)   110
(C)   120
(D)   130

16. Oskar recorded his 200-meter dash times for 10 consecutive days.

200-METER DASH TIMES FOR OCTOBER 18-27	
Oct 18	49.24 seconds
Oct 19	49.15 seconds
Oct 20	49.01 seconds
Oct 21	48.91 seconds
Oct 22	48.95 seconds
Oct 23	48.68 seconds
Oct 24	48.55 seconds
Oct 25	48.15 seconds
Oct 26	47.47 seconds
Oct 27	47.40 seconds

Oskar's time decreased for several days and then increased. On what day did Oskar's time increase?

(A)   Oct 22
(B)   Oct 23
(C)   Oct 24
(D)   Oct 25

17. The table shows how far Ximena ran in a certain amount of time.

Distance (miles)	Minutes
2	14
4	28
6	42
8	56
10	70
12	84

At her current rate, how far will Ximena run in 105 minutes?
(A)   13 miles
(B)   14 miles
(C)   15 miles
(D)   16 miles

18. The table below shows the results of 6 exams for two students.

Exam	Student 1	Student 2
1	Pass	Pass
2	Fail	Pass
3	Pass	Pass
4	Fail	Pass
5	Fail	Pass
6	Fail	Fail

What is the product of the number of tests passed by each of the two students?
(A)   4
(B)   6
(C)   8
(D)   10

19. The following table displays information about students' favorite colors.

Color	# of students
Purple	5
Red	4
Magenta	6
Green	8
Brown	1
Blue	3
Yellow	9

How many students preferred purple or brown, assuming none liked both?
(A)   5
(B)   6
(C)   7
(D)   8

20. Two schools, Spence and Chapin, competed on the number of community service projects their respective students could organize. Here are the results over 5 years:

Year	Spence	Chapin
1	6	9
2	7	2
3	2	4
4	5	8
5	3	3

How many total projects were completed by the school that won the competition?
(A)   23
(B)   26
(C)   29
(D)   32

21. The table shows how many pieces of music Davis plays on the piano in a certain amount of time.

Number of Pieces	Minutes
4	12
5	15
6	18
7	21

At his current rate, how many pieces can Davis play in 36 minutes?

(A)   8
(B)   9
(C)   11
(D)   12

22. A student recorded his 100-meter dash times for 10 consecutive days.

100-METER DASH TIMES FOR JUNE 16-25	
June 16	23.24 seconds
June 17	23.12 seconds
June 18	22.94 seconds
June 19	22.85 seconds
June 20	22.74 seconds
June 21	22.71 seconds
June 22	22.68 seconds
June 23	22.83 seconds
June 24	22.80 seconds
June 25	22.78 seconds

The student's time decreased for several days and then increased. On what day did the student's score increase?

(A)   June 23
(B)   June 24
(C)   June 25
(D)   June 26

23. The table shows how many pushups Zeinab can do in a certain amount of time.

Number of Pushups	Minutes
30	2
45	3
60	4
75	5

At her current rate, how many pushups can Zeinab do in 8 minutes?

(A)   100
(B)   120
(C)   140
(D)   160

24. The following table displays information about class pets.

Pet	# of students
Ferret	4
Cat	6
Rat	3
Horse	1
Chicken	2

How many students owned either a cat or a chicken, assuming none owned both?

(A)   8
(B)   9
(C)   10
(D)   11

25. Two salesmen, Dwight and Jim, competed to see who could sell the most reams of paper to their clients. Here are the results over 5 years:

Year	Dwight	Jim
1	15	12
2	12	13
3	14	9
4	8	10
5	12	13

How many total reams of paper were sold by the salesman that won the competition?

(A)   55
(B)   57
(C)   59
(D)   61

26. The table shows how many jumping jacks Jing can do in a certain amount of time.

Number of Jumping Jacks	Minutes
30	3
50	5
70	7
90	9

At her current rate, how many minutes will it take Jing to do 120 jumping jacks?

(A)   12
(B)   13
(C)   14
(D)   15

27. The table shows the number of copies made per minute with the school's new copy machine.

NEW COPY MACHINE	
Number of Copies	Minutes
25	5
50	10
75	15
100	20

A teacher needs to make 300 copies. How long will it take to make 300 copies?

(A)   25 minutes
(B)   40 minutes
(C)   60 minutes
(D)   80 minutes

28. The table below shows the results of 8 exams for two students.

Exam	Student 1	Student 2
1	Pass	Pass
2	Fail	Pass
3	Fail	Pass
4	Fail	Pass
5	Pass	Pass
6	Fail	Fail
7	Pass	Fail
8	Pass	Fail

What is the product of the number of exams passed by the two students?

(A)   8
(B)   12
(C)   16
(D)   20

Measurement

There isn't much strategy involved in *measurement* questions. If you have studied the units of measurement in Section III, these questions will be very easy!

Example #1
What units are most appropriate for measuring the length of a football field?
(A)   millimeters
(B)   meters
(C)   centimeters
(D)   kilograms

You're probably more familiar with some of these units than others. For example, even if you don't know exactly how long a centimeter is, you may know that 1 centimeter is pretty short; therefore, you definitely should *not* select (C) as your answer. If there are any other units of measurement that you recognize, and you also know they are not appropriate for measuring the length of a football field, then cross them off! **The correct answer is (B).** 1 meter is equal to approximately 3 feet. Millimeters are much too small to measure the length of a football field. Kilograms measure mass, not length.

Example #2
Amit was painting his room. How much paint did he most likely use?
(A)   2 milliliters
(B)   2 gallons
(C)   2 pounds
(D)   2 ounces

In this question, we need a measure of volume. Pounds measure weight, so cross off (C). Milliliters and ounces measure very small amounts of either volume or weight, respectively. Maybe you've seen a bucket of paint in your house or in a hardware store – do you remember how it was labeled? *Gallons* are the best unit of measurement, so **the correct answer is (B).**

Example #3
Shirley measured the width of her rectangular bedroom to be 12 feet and the length to be 13 feet. Using those measurements, which of the following could she **not** calculate?
(A)   The sum of the length and the width
(B)   The perimeter of her bedroom
(C)   The height of the ceiling
(D)   The area of her bedroom

The *sum* is the result of addition, and it is possible to add the length and the width. The perimeter of a rectangle is equal to $2l + 2w$, where l = length and w = width, both of which are given in this question. The equation for the area of a rectangle is *length* × *width*, both of which are given in this question. The only measure that Shirley cannot calculate is the height of the ceiling. **(C) is the correct answer.**

Practice Problems

1. Mohammed recorded a measurement of his notebook as 400 grams. Which notebook measurement did Mohammed record?
   (A)   length
   (B)   area
   (C)   weight
   (D)   volume

2. What is the best estimate for how many gallons of water are needed to fill the average kitchen sink?
   (A)   1
   (B)   10
   (C)   100
   (D)   1,000

3. A girl measured the width of her rectangular bedroom to be 8 feet and the length to be 9 feet. Using those measurements, which of the following could she not calculate?
   (A)   The difference between the length and width
   (B)   The perimeter of her bedroom
   (C)   The square footage of her bedroom
   (D)   The height of the walls

4. What units are most appropriate for measuring the weight of a person?
   (A)   kilograms
   (B)   grams
   (C)   feet
   (D)   meters

5. Ibrahim knows that a raisin weighs about one gram. Which object weighs about one kilogram?
   (A)   an elephant
   (B)   a person
   (C)   a car
   (D)   a hardcover book

6. Yu Yang poured milk for her bowl of cereal. How much milk did she likely pour?
   (A)   1 gallon
   (B)   1 liter
   (C)   1 ounce
   (D)   1 cup

7. A boy measured the area of his rectangular bedroom to be 40 square feet and the width to be 10 feet. Using those measurements, which of the following could he not calculate?
   (A)   The length of his bedroom
   (B)   The perimeter of his bedroom
   (C)   The difference between the length and width of his bedroom
   (D)   The number of windows in his bedroom

8. What is the best estimate for how many liters of water a bathtub holds?
   (A)   30
   (B)   300
   (C)   3,000
   (D)   30,000

9. Jesse recorded a measurement of his computer screen as 100 square inches. Which measurement did Jesse record?
   (A)   area
   (B)   length
   (C)   perimeter
   (D)   width

10. What units are most appropriate for measuring the volume of a swimming pool?
    (A)   ounces
    (B)   milliliters
    (C)   gallons
    (D)   feet

11. What is the best estimate for how much a car weighs?
   (A)   50 kilograms
   (B)   4,000 pounds
   (C)   200 ounces
   (D)   1,000 gallons

12. A boy measured the perimeter of his rectangular bedroom to be 36 feet and the length to be 8 feet. Using those measurements, which of the following could he not calculate?
   (A)   The height of the ceiling
   (B)   The width of his bedroom
   (C)   The area of his bedroom
   (D)   The sum of the length and width

13. Santiago knows that the width of the average pinkie finger is about one centimeter. Which object is about one meter long?
   (A)   a computer screen
   (B)   a TV remote control
   (C)   a notebook
   (D)   the width of a doorway

14. What is the best estimate for the length of a tree leaf?
   (A)   5 centimeters
   (B)   5 feet
   (C)   5 meters
   (D)   5 millimeters

15. A girl measured the width of her rectangular bedroom to be 14 feet and the length to be 8 feet. Using those measurements, which of the following could she not calculate?
   (B)   The difference between the length and width
   (B)   The height of the ceiling
   (C)   The area of her bedroom
   (D)   The perimeter of her bedroom

16. Amir was watering a house plant. How much water did he most likely use?
   (A)   0.1 ounces
   (B)   10 ounces
   (C)   100 ounces
   (D)   1,000 ounces

17. Keira recorded a measurement of her door frame as 85 inches. Which measurement did Keira record?
   (A)   area
   (B)   length
   (C)   weight
   (D)   volume

18. What units are most appropriate for measuring the height of a tree?
   (A)   centimeters
   (B)   inches
   (C)   meters
   (D)   gallons

19. About how much shampoo does a shampoo bottle most likely hold?
   (A)   1 ounce
   (B)   16 ounces
   (C)   160 ounces
   (D)   1,600 ounces

20. Ahmed knows that a stick of gum weighs about one gram. Which object weighs about one kilogram?
   (A)   a small cantaloupe
   (B)   a large dog
   (C)   a flat screen TV
   (D)   a cell phone

21. Shane recorded a measurement of his fingernail as 7 millimeters. Which measurement did Shane record?
   (A)   area
   (B)   length
   (C)   weight
   (D)   volume

Perimeter and Area Questions

The most important thing to do on *perimeter and area questions* is pay attention to what the question is asking. If you are asked to find perimeter, the answer choices will often include the shape's area; if the question asks for area, the answer choices will often include the shape's perimeter. It's very easy to make careless mistakes on these questions.

Example #1

The figure shows a drawing of Mark's bedroom

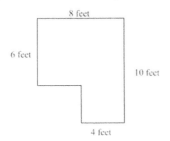

What is the perimeter of Mark's bedroom?
(A)   20 feet
(B)   28 feet
(C)   36 feet
(D)   80 feet

There are two ways of approaching this problem. The harder way is to find the lengths of the missing sides and then add up the 6 different lengths to find the total perimeter. If the total width of the bedroom is 8 feet, and 4 feet are accounted for on the southern end of the bedroom, then the length of the other horizontal section must also be 4 feet (because 8 – 4 = 4). If the width of the bedroom is 10 feet, and 6 feet are accounted for on the western side of the bedroom, then the length of the other vertical section must be 4 feet (because 10 – 6 = 4). Then, add everything together: 8 + 10 + 4 + 4 + 4 + 6 = 36. **The correct answer is (C).**

The other way you can complete these questions is to look at the long edges (here, those edges are 8 and 10 feet). The length across from 8 feet will also be a total of 8 feet, and the width across from 10 feet will also be a total of 10 feet, so you can simply find the sum of 8 + 8 + 10 + 10.

Example #2

The figure shows a drawing of Brad's bedroom.

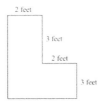

What is the area of Brad's bedroom?
(A)   12 square feet
(B)   18 square feet
(C)   24 square feet
(D)   30 square feet

In this question, you are asked to find area. These questions are a little trickier because you'll need to split the L-shape into two pieces:

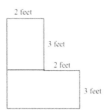

The upper piece is 2 feet by 3 feet, while the lower piece is 3 feet by 4 feet. Where did the 4 come from? You can see that the two horizontal pieces are each 2 feet long. 2 + 2 = 4, so the bottom side of the shape must be 4 feet long. Now, you simply find the area of each shape and add them together. 6 + 12 = 18, so **the correct answer is (B).**

Example #3

Ms. Grabot's dining room table can be lengthened by adding a 5-foot wide, 15-foot long section to the middle of it.

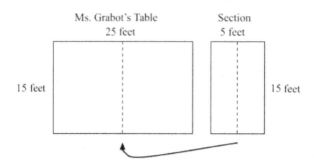

What will happen to the perimeter of Ms. Grabot's table if she adds the 5-foot wide, 15-foot long section to the middle?

(A)   It will increase by 5 feet

(B)   It will increase by 10 feet

(C)   It will increase by 20 feet

(D)   It will increase by 40 feet

Remember, perimeter measures the length of the *outside* of an object. If you place the section in the middle of the table, how many sides of the section will be included when measuring perimeter? Only the top and bottom, because the vertical sides will be *within* the table. The length will increase by 10, so **the correct answer is (B)**. If the section were added to the right or left side of the table, the perimeter would still increase by only 10 feet, because the top and bottom of the section would be the only new portions included in the new perimeter.

You may be asked a similar question about area. Since area measures the *inside* of a shape, and the area of this section is 75 square feet, the total area of the table will increase by 75 square feet no matter where you place the section: in the middle of the table, on the side of the table, etc.

Example #4

A triangle has side lengths of 3, 4, and 5. If each side of the triangle is tripled, what is the perimeter of the triangle?

(A)   12

(B)   24

(C)   36

(D)   48

This question is easy; you just have to read the directions carefully. To find the perimeter of a shape, add up all of the sides. Tripling the length of each of the given sides results in side lengths of 9, 12, and 15. Then, find the sum. $9 + 12 + 15 = 36$. **(C) is the correct answer.**

Practice Problems

1. Mr. Smith's dining room table can be lengthened by adding a 2-foot wide, 4-foot long section to the middle of it.

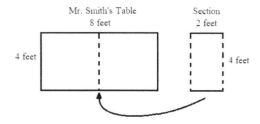

   What will happen to the perimeter of Mr. Smith's table if he adds the 2-foot wide, 4-foot long section to the middle?
   (A)   It will increase by 2 feet
   (B)   It will increase by 4 feet
   (C)   It will increase by 6 feet
   (D)   It will increase by 8 feet

2. A rectangle has a width of 5 inches and a length of 7 inches. If the width and the length of the rectangle are doubled, what is the rectangle's perimeter?
   (A)   24 inches
   (B)   36 inches
   (C)   48 inches
   (D)   60 inches

3. The figure shows a drawing of Miguel's bedroom.

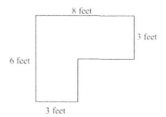

   What is the area of Miguel's bedroom?
   (A)   10 square feet
   (B)   14 square feet
   (C)   33 square feet
   (D)   48 square feet

4. Mrs. Yarbrough's dining room table can be lengthened by adding a 4-foot wide, 7-foot long section to the middle of it.

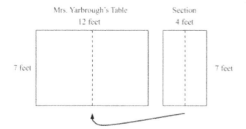

   What will happen to the area of Mrs. Yarbrough's table if she adds the 4-foot wide, 7-foot long section to the middle?
   (A)   It will increase by 4 square feet
   (B)   It will increase by 8 square feet
   (C)   It will increase by 11 square feet
   (D)   It will increase by 28 square feet

5. A triangle has side lengths of 5, 7, and 9. If each side of the triangle is doubled, what is the triangle's perimeter?
   (A)   21
   (B)   26
   (C)   41
   (D)   42

6. A man is planning his new garden, and he has four different options for its dimensions. Which one will give him the most space to grow his vegetables?
   (A)   4 feet × 4 feet
   (B)   5 feet × 2 feet
   (C)   6 feet × 1 foot
   (D)   3 feet × 5 feet

7. The length of one side of a square is 5 feet. What is the square's area?
   (A)   5 square feet
   (B)   10 square feet
   (C)   20 square feet
   (D)   25 square feet

8. A rectangle has a width of 4 inches and a length of 5 inches. If the width and the length of the rectangle are tripled, what is the rectangle's area?
    (A)   180 square inches
    (B)   190 square inches
    (C)   200 square inches
    (D)   210 square inches

9. Mr. Klein's dining room table can be lengthened by adding a 1-foot wide, 3-foot long section to the middle of it.

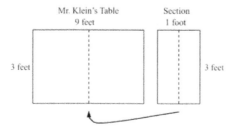

    What will happen to the area of Mr. Klein's table if he adds the 1-foot wide, 3-foot long section to the middle?
    (A)   It will increase by 2 square feet
    (B)   It will increase by 3 square feet
    (C)   It will increase by 4 square feet
    (D)   It will increase by 8 square feet

10. A triangle has side lengths of 4, 4, and 7. If each side of the triangle is doubled, what is the triangle's perimeter?
    (A)   15
    (B)   30
    (C)   35
    (D)   40

11. A woman is planning her new garden, and she has four different options for its dimensions. Which one will give her the most space to grow her vegetables?
    (A)   15 feet × 4 feet
    (B)   10 feet × 7 feet
    (C)   11 feet × 6 feet
    (D)   9 feet × 8 feet

12. The figure shows a drawing of Marty's bedroom

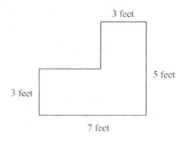

    What is the area of Marty's bedroom?
    (A)   18 square feet
    (B)   24 square feet
    (C)   27 square feet
    (D)   35 square feet

13. A rectangle has a length of 3 inches and a width of 10 inches. What is the rectangle's perimeter?
    (A)   13 inches
    (B)   26 inches
    (C)   30 inches
    (D)   36inches

14. Mr. Singh's dining room table can be lengthened by adding a 2-foot wide, 4-foot long section to the side of it.

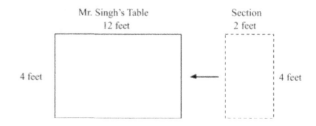

    What will happen to the area of Mr. Singh's table if he adds the 2-foot wide, 4-foot long section to the table's side?
    (A)   It will increase by 4 square feet
    (B)   It will increase by 6 square feet
    (C)   It will increase by 8 square feet
    (D)   It will increase by 10 square feet

15. The area of the rectangle shown below is 63 square centimeters. What is the length of side x?

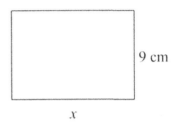

9 cm

x

(A)   7 cm
(B)   8 cm
(C)   9 cm
(D)   10 cm

16. A man is planning his new garden, and he has four different options for its dimensions. Which one will give him the most space to grow his vegetables?
(A)   8 feet × 4 feet
(B)   6 feet × 6 feet
(C)   31 feet × 1 foot
(D)   5 feet × 7 feet

17. The figure shows a drawing of Manuel's bedroom

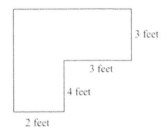

3 feet

3 feet

4 feet

2 feet

What is the perimeter of Manuel's bedroom?
(A)   24 feet
(B)   25 feet
(C)   26 feet
(D)   27 feet

18. A rectangle has a width of 7 inches and a length of 9 inches. If the width and the length of the rectangle are doubled, what is the rectangle's perimeter?
(A)   64 inches
(B)   65 inches
(C)   66 inches
(D)   67 inches

19. The figure shows a drawing of Kimmy's bedroom.

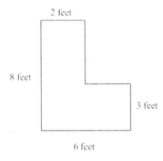

2 feet

8 feet

3 feet

6 feet

What is the perimeter of Kimmy's bedroom?
(A)   19 feet
(B)   23 feet
(C)   26 feet
(D)   28 feet

20. The area of the rectangle shown below is 60 square cm. What is the length of side x?

12 cm

x

(A)   5 cm
(B)   8 cm
(C)   18 cm
(D)   20 cm

21. A triangle has side lengths of 10, 11, and 12. If each side of the triangle is tripled, what is the triangle's perimeter?
(A)   32
(B)   33
(C)   66
(D)   99

22. A rectangle is 7 feet by 6 feet. What is the rectangle's perimeter?
    (A)   22 feet
    (B)   26 feet
    (C)   36 feet
    (D)   42 feet

23. Ms. Argerich's dining room table can be lengthened by adding a 5-foot wide, 15-foot long section to the side of it.

    What will happen to the perimeter of Ms. Argerich's table if she adds the 5-foot wide, 15-foot long section to the side?
    (A)   It will increase by 10 feet
    (B)   It will increase by 20 feet
    (C)   It will increase by 25 feet
    (D)   It will increase by 40 feet

24. The figure shows a drawing of Charlie's bedroom

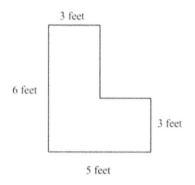

    What is the perimeter of Charlie's bedroom?
    (A)   17 feet
    (B)   22 feet
    (C)   24 feet
    (D)   30 feet

25. A triangle has side lengths of 8, 12, and 14. If each side of the triangle is halved, what is the triangle's perimeter?
    (A)   17
    (B)   34
    (C)   68
    (D)   70

26. Ms. Buttera's dining room table can be lengthened by adding a 1-foot wide, 3-foot long section to the side of it.

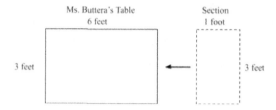

    What will happen to the perimeter of Ms. Buttera's table if she adds the 1-foot wide, 3-foot long section to the side?
    (A)   It will increase by 2 feet
    (B)   It will increase by 3 feet
    (C)   It will increase by 5 feet
    (D)   It will increase by 8 feet

27. The rectangle below has a perimeter of 28 cm. What is the length of side x?

    (A)   4 cm
    (B)   5 cm
    (C)   7 cm
    (D)   10 cm

28. A woman is planning her new garden, and she has four different options for its dimensions. Which one will give her the most space to grow her vegetables?
    (A)   7 feet × 7 feet
    (B)   9 feet × 5 feet
    (C)   12 feet × 4 feet
    (D)   3 feet × 15 feet

29. A rectangle has a width of 10 inches and a length of 12 inches. If the width and the length of the rectangle are halved, what is the rectangle's area?
    (A)   20 square inches
    (B)   30 square inches
    (C)   35 square inches
    (D)   40 square inches

30. A rectangle has a width of 20 inches and a length of 16 inches. If the width and the length of the rectangle are halved, what is the rectangle's perimeter?
    (A)   16 inches
    (B)   18 inches
    (C)   34 inches
    (D)   36 inches

31. A triangle has side lengths of 10, 12, and 12. If each side of the triangle is halved, what is the triangle's perimeter?
    (A)   16
    (B)   17
    (C)   32
    (D)   34

32. A man is planning his new garden, and he has four different options for its dimensions. Which one will give him the most space to grow his vegetables?
    (A)   7 feet × 6 feet
    (B)   8 feet × 5 feet
    (C)   12 feet × 4 feet
    (D)   3 feet × 15 feet

Patterns

You never know what type of shape or figure you'll be presented with on a *patterns* question, so you must train yourself to be able to identify patterns in a variety of situations.

Example #1
A pattern is shown below.

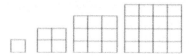

How many squares will there be in the 5th figure?
(A)   16
(B)   25
(C)   30
(D)   36

You can see that there are 4 figures presented in the pattern. Since you are asked to find the 5th figure, you simply need to identify what the next shape will look like. In this pattern, the length and width of the larger squares increase by one in each successive figure. Therefore, the next square will be 5 × 5. The equation for area is length × width, so the area of the 5th figure is 5 × 5 = 25. **The correct answer is (B).** The 6th figure would have 36 squares, so (D) is a trick answer.

Example #2
A pattern is shown below.

What will the 8th shape in the pattern be?

(A)

(B)

(C)

(D)

The pattern in this figure is difficult to identify. It goes "circle, heart, circle, heart," so you know the 8th shape will be a heart. You can eliminate (A) and (B). It looks like the color pattern is "2 black, 2 white, 2 black, 2 white," but the pattern has started in the middle, which is why there is only one black shape at the beginning. The 8th shape will be black, so **the correct answer is (D).**

Example #3

What is the next number in the sequence?

7, 2, -3, -8, ___

(A)   -13
(B)   -12
(C)   12
(D)   13

You probably have not studied negative numbers in 3rd grade, but it's still possible to narrow down the answer choices on this question! First, you should notice that the numbers start positive but then become negative. This means the next number in the sequence will probably also be negative. Then, do 7 – 2 = 5. Those two numbers are 5 apart on the number line. You may not know how to find how far apart 2 and -3 are, but that's okay: let's just assume that all the numbers are 5 apart.

Once you get to -3 and -8 in the sequence, you'll notice that the number after the negative sign increases. What number is 5 away from 8? 8 + 5 = 13. Remember to put the negative sign in front of that to get -13. **The correct answer is (A).**

Example #4

What fraction is missing in the pattern?

$\frac{1}{2}$, $\frac{3}{4}$, ___, $1\frac{1}{4}$

(A) $\frac{1}{4}$

(B) $\frac{3}{8}$

(C)   1

(D) $1\frac{1}{2}$

To answer this question, you'll need to be comfortable with reducing and manipulating fractions. First, convert $\frac{1}{2}$ to $\frac{2}{4}$. Then, it's easier to compare $\frac{2}{4}$ to $\frac{3}{4}$. You can see that the sequence increases by $\frac{1}{4}$

$\frac{3}{4} + \frac{1}{4} = \frac{4}{4}$ or 1, so **(C) is the correct answer.** This is a tough question. If you're stuck, you should at least eliminate (D), since it's too big, and then guess from the remaining answer choices!

Practice Problems

1. Dana used a rule to make a number pattern. Her rule is to multiply by 2. Which number pattern follows Dana's rule?
    (A)   4, 6, 8, 10, 12
    (B)   2, 4, 8, 16, 32
    (C)   5, 7, 9, 11, 13
    (D)   2, 4, 8, 15, 20

2. A pattern is shown below.

    What will the next figure in this pattern be?

    (A)   ■ ☐ ☐

    (B)   ☐ ☐ ■

    (C)   ☐ ■ ☐

    (D)   ☐ ☐ ☐

3. A pattern is shown below.

    1, 2, 4, 7, 11, 16, 22, ?

    What will the next number in the pattern be?
    (A)   29
    (B)   30
    (C)   31
    (D)   32

4. What number is missing in the pattern?

    12, 16, _____, 24, 28

    (A)   17
    (B)   20
    (C)   29
    (D)   32

5. What is the next number in the sequence?

    4, 1, -2, -5, ___

    (A)   -8
    (B)   -7
    (C)   7
    (D)   8

6. What fraction is missing in the pattern?

    $\frac{1}{6}$, $\frac{1}{3}$, $\frac{1}{2}$, ____

    (A) $\frac{1}{4}$

    (B) $\frac{2}{4}$

    (C) $\frac{2}{3}$

    (D) $\frac{3}{4}$

7. A pattern is shown below.

    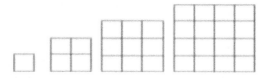

    How many squares will there be in the 6th figure?
    (A)   25
    (B)   36
    (C)   49
    (D)   64

8. What is the next number in the sequence?

    -8, -4, 0, 4, ___

    (A) 5
    (B) 6
    (C) 7
    (D) 8

9. A subtraction rule was used to make the pattern of numbers in the table.

31	29	27	25	23	?	?

    If the pattern continues, what would the next two numbers be?
    (A) 25, 27
    (B) 22, 21
    (C) 21, 19
    (D) 24, 25

10. What fraction is missing in the pattern?

    $\frac{1}{2}$, ___, 1, $1\frac{1}{4}$

    (A) $\frac{1}{4}$
    (B) $\frac{3}{4}$
    (C) $\frac{1}{6}$
    (D) $\frac{2}{3}$

11. What is the next number in the sequence?

    9, 1, -7, -15, ___

    (A) -23
    (B) -22
    (C) 22
    (D) 23

12. A pattern is shown below.

    What will the next shape in the pattern be?

    (A) ◯

    (B) ●

    (C) ♡

    (D) ♥

13. What are the missing numbers in the pattern below?

    21, 24, ____, ____, 33, _____

    (A) 25, 26, 34
    (B) 26, 28, 34
    (C) 27, 29, 35
    (D) 27, 30, 36

14. A pattern is shown below.

    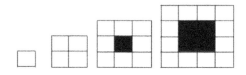

    How many squares will be shaded in the 5th figure?
    (A) 6
    (B) 7
    (C) 8
    (D) 9

15. What fraction is missing in the pattern?

$$\frac{1}{10}, \quad \frac{1}{5}, \quad \frac{3}{10}, \quad \underline{\quad}$$

(A) $\frac{2}{10}$

(B) $\frac{2}{5}$

(C) $\frac{1}{2}$

(D) $\frac{3}{5}$

16. Sally is selling candy bars for her school.

Day	Bars Sold
Monday	3
Tuesday	6
Wednesday	9
Thursday	?

If the pattern continues, how many candy bars will Sally sell on Thursday?
(A)   3
(B)   10
(C)   11
(D)   12

17. Jaime made a pattern using a two-step rule in which he first multiplies and then subtracts. His pattern is shown below:

7, 14, 11, 22, 19, 38, 35, 70, ?

What is the next number in the pattern?
(A)   61
(B)   64
(C)   67
(D)   140

18. What is the next number in the sequence?

-5, -1, 3, 7, ___

(A)   9
(B)   10
(C)   11
(D)   12

19. A pattern is shown below.

What will the 8ᵗʰ figure in this pattern be?

(A) ■ □ □

(B) □ □ ■

(C) □ ■ □

(D) □ □ □

20. A student used a rule to create the following pattern:

15, 19, 23, 27, 31, 35

Her friend created a similar pattern using the same rule. Which pattern did her friend create?
(A)   4, 8, 12, 16, 20
(B)   5, 9, 13, 15, 17
(C)   2, 4, 8, 16, 32
(D)   14, 19, 24, 29, 34

21. A number pattern is shown below:

    50, 45, 65, 60, 80, 75, 95, ?

    If the pattern continues, what number will come next?
    (A)   75
    (B)   90
    (C)   100
    (D)   105

22. A student is collecting plastic bottles on the beach. She puts 24 bottles in her first bag, 33 bottles in her second bag, 42 bottles in her third bag, and 51 bottles in her fourth bag. If this pattern continues, how many bottles will the student put in her sixth bag?
    (A)   58
    (B)   60
    (C)   69
    (D)   75

23. What are the missing numbers in the pattern below?

    15, 24, ____, ____, 51, _____

    (A)   29, 39, 60
    (B)   33, 40, 59
    (C)   33, 42, 60
    (D)   34, 44, 64

24. What fraction is missing in the pattern?

    $$\frac{1}{8}, \quad \text{\_\_\_}, \quad \frac{3}{8}, \quad \frac{1}{2}$$

    (A) $\frac{1}{16}$

    (B) $\frac{4}{8}$

    (C) $\frac{3}{4}$

    (D) $\frac{1}{4}$

25. Collette is selling brownies at the school bake sale.

Day	Bars Sold
Monday 1/11	8
Tuesday 1/12	16
Wednesday 1/13	24
Thursday 1/14	?

    Collette will sell twice as many brownies on Thursday, 1/21 as she does on Thursday, 1/14. How many brownies will she sell on Thursday, 1/21?
    (A)   16
    (B)   32
    (C)   48
    (D)   64

26. A pattern is shown below:

    10, 14, 22, 38, 70, ?

    What will the next number in this pattern be?
    (A)   134
    (B)   138
    (C)   142
    (D)   146

27. A pattern is shown below.

    How many small squares will there be in the 8th figure?
    (A)   25
    (B)   36
    (C)   49
    (D)   64

Scales

Scales questions can be tricky. They usually show a balanced scale and ask you how much objects on the scale must weigh in relation to one another.

Example #1

The figure shows Carlos and Samuel's containers.

Samuel   Carlos

If each scale is balanced, which diagram shows that Carlos's container weighs 1 pound more than Samuel's container? Let 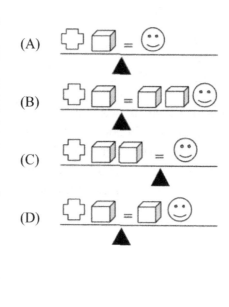 = 1 pound.

Let's go through these answer choices one by one. Note that the cubes each weigh one pound. For the scale in (A) to be balanced, one pound had to be added to Carlos's side. That means that Carlos's container weighs one pound *less* than Samuel's container. To make this easier to visualize, you can assign a weight to the containers. For example, let's say Samuel's container weighs 5 pounds. That means there are 5 pounds on the right side of the scale. On the left side, you know that the cube weighs 1 pound. That means Carlos's container must weigh 4 pounds, since 4 + 1 = 5, and this would balance the scale.

In answer choice (B), cross out one cube on both sides of the scale. You can do this because each cube weighs one pound, so they cancel each other out. This leaves you with one cube on the right side of the scale. Based on the work you did for (A), you know that Samuel's container weighs one pound less than Carlos's container. In other words, Carlos's container weighs one pound *more* than Samuel's container. **(B) is the correct answer**.

In (C), Carlos's container weighs two pounds less than Samuel's container. In (D), both containers weigh the same amount.

Practice Problems

1. The figure shows Alex and Jack's containers.

    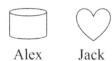

    If each scale is balanced, which diagram shows that Alex's container weighs 2 pounds more than Jack's container? Let = 1 pound.

    (A)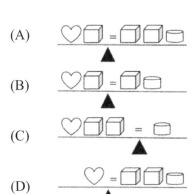

    (B)

    (C)

    (D)

2. The figure shows Zahid and Feng's containers.

    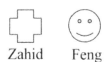

    If each scale is balanced, which diagram shows that Zahid's container weighs 2 pounds more than Feng's container? Let = 2 pounds.

    (A)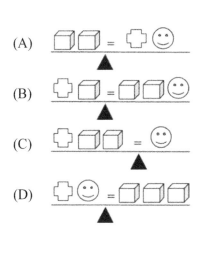

    (B)

    (C)

    (D)

3. The figure shows Selma and Omar's containers.

    If each scale is balanced, which diagram shows that Selma's container weighs the same as Omar's container? Let = 1 pound.

    (A)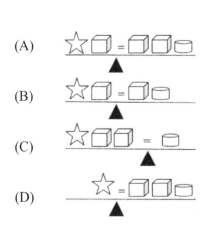

    (B)

    (C)

    (D)

4. The figure shows Logan and Nareh's containers.

Logan   Nareh

If each scale is balanced, which diagram shows that Logan's container weighs 4 pounds less than Nareh's container? Let ⬛ = 2 pounds.

(A)

(B)

(C)

(D)

5. The figure shows Nicola and Gustav's containers.

Nicola   Gustav

If each scale is balanced, which diagram shows that Gustav's container weighs 1 pound more than Nicola's container? Let ⬛ = 1 pound.

(A)

(B)

(C)

(D)

6. The figure shows Ivan and Aloysha's containers.

Ivan   Aloysha

If each scale is balanced, which diagram shows that the combined weight of Ivan and Aloysha's containers is 6 pounds? Let ⬛ = 3 pounds.

(A)

(B)

(C)

(D)

7. The figure shows Martine and
    Nathalie's containers.

    Martine   Nathalie

    If each scale is balanced, which diagram
    shows that Martine's container weighs 2
    pounds more than Nathalie's container?
    Let ⬡ = 1 pound.

    (A)
    (B)
    (C)
    (D)

8. The figure shows Delwin and Lin's
    containers.

    Delwin   Lin

    If each scale is balanced, which diagram
    shows that Delwin's container weighs 4
    pounds less than Lin's container? Let
    ⬡ = 2 pounds.

    (A)
    (B)
    (C)
    (D)

Function Machines

Function machines show the relationship between input and output.

Example #1

Determine what rule the function machine is using.

In	Out
20	10
26	16
38	28
52	42

(A)   Add 6
(B)   Subtract 6
(C)   Add 10
(D)   Subtract 10

When working on function tables, you must determine the relationship between what goes in and what comes out. In the table to the left, when 20 goes in, 10 comes out. When 26 goes in, 16 comes out. Notice that the second number is 10 less than the first number in both instances. That means that you must subtract 10 to find the relationship between the two columns. **The correct answer is (D).**

These questions may contain trick answers. If you look only at the left column, you might think the relationship is add 6, because 26 is 6 greater than 20. Don't make this common mistake! Remember, you must find the relationship between the left and the right columns.

Example #2

Use the table to determine the rule.

Input ▲	Output ■
4	9
7	15
10	21
12	25

What is the rule for the function?
(A) $\blacktriangle + 5 = \blacksquare$
(B) $\blacktriangle \times 2 + 1 = \blacksquare$
(C) $\blacktriangle \times 3 - 3 = \blacksquare$
(D) $\blacktriangle + 3 = \blacksquare$

This question is a little trickier. Plug in a number from the Input side of the table into each equation, and see which equation pops out the correct number on the Output side. These questions will always contain trick answers, so you need to test at least two of the numbers on the Input side before selecting an answer. (A) works when the input is 4, because $4 + 5 = 9$. However, when you try it with 7, you'll see that $7 + 5 \neq 15$, so (A) is incorrect. **(B) is the correct answer.**

Practice Problems

1. Determine what rule the function machine is using.

In	Out
20	15
26	21
38	33
52	47

(A)   Add 6
(B)   Subtract 6
(C)   Add 5
(D)   Subtract 5

2. Use the table to determine the rule.

Input ▲	Output ■
0	2
15	17
17	19
22	24

What is the rule for the function?
(A) $▲ + 13 = ■$
(B) $▲ - 4 = ■$
(C) $▲ + 2 = ■$
(D) $▲ × 0 + 2 = ■$

3. Determine what rule the function machine is using.

In	Out
19	15
27	23
32	28
33	29
36	32

(A)   Subtract 4
(B)   Subtract 6
(C)   Add 4
(D)   Subtract 1

4. Use the table to determine the rule.

Input ▲	Output ■
8	0
16	2
20	3
44	9

What is the rule for the function?
(A) $▲ - 8 = ■$
(B) $▲ + 8 = ■$
(C) $(▲ × 2) - 16 = ■$
(D) $▲ ÷ 4 - 2 = ■$

5. Determine what rule the function machine is using.

In	Out
11	22
23	34
35	46
43	54

(A)   Add 12
(B)   Subtract 12
(C)   Add 11
(D)   Subtract 11

6. Use the table to determine the rule.

Input ▲	Output ■
0	0
1	3
9	27
12	36

What is the rule for the function?
(A) $▲ × 3 = ■$
(B) $▲ + 0 = ■$
(C) $▲ + 1 = ■$
(D) $▲ ÷ 3 = ■$

7. Determine what rule the function machine is using.

In	Out
19	12
21	14
30	23
46	39

(A)   Add 9
(B)   Subtract 5
(C)   Subtract 7
(D)   Add 7

8. Use the table to determine the rule.

Input ▲	Output ■
1	1
4	16
6	36
8	64

What is the rule for the function?
(A) $\blacktriangle \times 1 = \blacksquare$
(B) $\blacktriangle + 3 = \blacksquare$
(C) $\blacktriangle + 5 = \blacksquare$
(D) $\blacktriangle \times \blacktriangle = \blacksquare$

9. Use the table to determine the rule.

Input ▲	Output ■
10	15
16	24
22	33
26	39

What is the rule for the function?
(A) $\blacktriangle \div 2 + \blacktriangle = \blacksquare$
(B) $\blacktriangle + 5 = \blacksquare$
(C) $\blacktriangle + 6 \div \blacktriangle = \blacksquare$
(D) $\blacktriangle \div 2 = \blacksquare$

10. Determine what rule the function machine is using.

In	Out
20	16
22	18
23	19
42	38
44	40

(A)   Subtract 4
(B)   Add 6
(C)   Subtract 6
(D)   Add 4

11. Use the table to determine the rule.

Input ▲	Output ■
6	10
10	18
13	24
15	28

What is the rule for the function?
(A) $\blacktriangle + 4 = \blacksquare$
(B) $\blacktriangle - 2 + \blacktriangle = \blacksquare$
(C) $(\blacktriangle - 2) \times 2 = \blacksquare$
(D) $\blacktriangle \times 2 + \blacktriangle = \blacksquare$

12. Determine what rule the function machine is using.

In	Out
4	12
7	21
15	45
20	60

(A)   Add 3
(B)   Add 8
(C)   Times 3
(D)   Divided by 3

13. Determine what rule the function machine is using.

In	Out
4	0
9	0
11	0
24	0
32	0

(A)   Minus 4
(B)   Plus 5
(C)   Times 0
(D)   Times 1

14. Determine what rule the function machine is using.

In	Out
6	2
15	5
24	8
30	10
33	11

(A)   Plus 6
(B)   Minus 4
(C)   Times 3
(D)   Divided by 3

Fractions

Fractions questions may test you on basic knowledge of adding, subtracting, multiplying, or dividing fractions, or they may present you with a figure or word problem. You must always remember that a fraction represents "part out of whole." These questions often contain trick answers.

Example #1

What fraction of the figure below is shaded?

(A) $\frac{1}{12}$

(B) $\frac{4}{8}$

(C) $\frac{8}{12}$

(D) $\frac{1}{3}$

First, note that the question asks about the *shaded* part of the figure. There are 4 shaded squares, and 12 squares total. The fraction should be $\frac{4}{12}$, but that's not an option. Try reducing the fraction. 4 and 12 are both divisible by 3, so the fraction can be reduced to $\frac{1}{3}$. **(D) is the correct answer**. (C) is a trick answer – it represents the unshaded portion of the figure. (B) contains a common misconception. It represents shaded squares over unshaded squares.

Example #2

Jeffrey brought some pieces of candy to school. He gave $\frac{1}{4}$ of the candy to his friend Jack, and $\frac{1}{2}$ of the candy to his teacher. If Jack got 4 pieces of candy from Jeffrey, how many pieces of candy does Jeffrey have now?

(A)   4
(B)   8
(C)   12
(D)   16

This is a very difficult question. To answer it, you need to figure out how many pieces of candy Jeffrey had when he got to school. Jack got 4 pieces of candy, which was $\frac{1}{4}$ of Jeffrey's total candy. 4 pieces is $\frac{1}{4}$ of how many total pieces? You may have to think about this for a while. $\frac{1}{4}$ of 4 is 1, so 4 is definitely not enough. $\frac{1}{4}$ of 12 is 3, so that's still not quite enough. $\frac{1}{4}$ of 16 is 4, so you know that Jeffrey brought 16 pieces of candy to school. That means he must have given 8 pieces to his teacher. 16 − 8 − 4 = 4, so Jeffrey has 4 pieces of candy left. **(A) is the correct answer**. (B) represents how many pieces of candy Jeffrey gave to his teacher; (C) shows how many pieces he gave away in total, and (D) is the number of pieces he started with. Make sure you choose the answer that addresses what the question asks!

Example #3

Which fraction is between $\frac{1}{2}$ and $\frac{6}{8}$?

(A) $\frac{1}{3}$

(B) $\frac{4}{8}$

(C) $\frac{5}{8}$

(D) $\frac{9}{10}$

There's a strategy for these questions. If possible, change the fractions in the question stem so that they both have the same denominator. $\frac{1 \times 4}{2 \times 4} = \frac{4}{8}$. Once you've done this, it becomes obvious that the fraction between $\frac{4}{8}$ and $\frac{6}{8}$ is $\frac{5}{8}$, so **the correct answer is (C).**

Practice Problems

1. Florencia brought some pieces of candy to school. She gave $\frac{1}{6}$ of the candy to her friend Isadora, and $\frac{4}{6}$ of the candy to her teacher. If Isadora got 1 piece of candy from Florencia, how many pieces of candy does Florencia have now?

    (A)   1
    (B)   2
    (C)   3
    (D)   4

2. What fraction of the figure below is shaded?

    (A) $\frac{5}{11}$

    (B) $\frac{1}{4}$

    (C) $\frac{5}{16}$

    (D) $\frac{1}{3}$

3. Ori brought some pieces of candy to school. He gave $\frac{2}{6}$ of the candy to his friend Hydar, and $\frac{1}{6}$ of the candy to his teacher. If Hydar got 2 pieces of candy from Ori, how many pieces of candy does Ori have now?

    (A)   1
    (B)   2
    (C)   3
    (D)   4

4. Which fraction is between $\frac{1}{6}$ and $\frac{5}{6}$?

    (A) $\frac{1}{6}$

    (B) $\frac{2}{3}$

    (C) $\frac{9}{10}$

    (D) $\frac{7}{6}$

5. Lara created the design below.

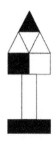

What fraction of the shapes in her design is shaded?

(A) $\frac{3}{8}$

(B) $\frac{5}{3}$

(C) $\frac{3}{5}$

(D) $\frac{8}{3}$

6. Which fraction is between $\frac{1}{5}$ and $\frac{8}{10}$?

(A) $\frac{1}{10}$

(B) $\frac{3}{5}$

(C) $\frac{9}{10}$

(D) $\frac{19}{20}$

7. Xiaoyan brought some pieces of candy to school. She gave $\frac{1}{8}$ of the candy to her friend Jesse, and $\frac{3}{8}$ of the candy to her teacher. If Jesse got 1 piece of candy from Xiaoyan, how many pieces of candy did her teacher get?

(A)   1
(B)   2
(C)   3
(D)   4

8. Which fraction is the least?

(A) $\frac{5}{9}$

(B) $\frac{3}{7}$

(C) $\frac{6}{11}$

(D) $\frac{7}{13}$

9. Which fraction is the greatest?

(A) $\frac{6}{11}$

(B) $\frac{2}{11}$

(C) $\frac{5}{11}$

(D) $\frac{7}{11}$

10. What fraction of the figure below is shaded?

(A) $\frac{4}{12}$

(B) $\frac{1}{3}$

(C) $\frac{1}{4}$

(D) $\frac{5}{16}$

11. Which fraction is between $\frac{3}{4}$ and $\frac{15}{16}$?

(A) $\frac{2}{8}$

(B) $\frac{1}{2}$

(C) $\frac{19}{20}$

(D) $\frac{7}{8}$

12. Robin brought some pieces of candy to school. She gave $\frac{1}{4}$ of the candy to her friend Aron, and $\frac{1}{2}$ of the candy to her teacher. If Aron got 2 pieces of candy from Robin, how many pieces of candy does Robin have now?

    (A)   2
    (B)   3
    (C)   4
    (D)   8

13. Which fraction is between $\frac{1}{2}$ and $\frac{3}{4}$?

    (A) $\frac{1}{4}$
    (B) $\frac{3}{5}$
    (C) $\frac{4}{5}$
    (D) $\frac{7}{8}$

14. Elias brought some pieces of candy to school. He gave $\frac{1}{3}$ of the candy to his friend Filip, and $\frac{1}{2}$ of the candy to his teacher. If the teacher got 12 pieces of candy from Elias, how many pieces of candy did Filip get?

    (A)   4
    (B)   8
    (C)   9
    (D)   12

15. What portion of the figure below is shaded?

    (A) $\frac{6}{16}$
    (B) $\frac{4}{8}$
    (C) $\frac{3}{8}$
    (D) $\frac{8}{8}$

16. Which fraction is between $\frac{9}{10}$ and 1 ?

    (A) $\frac{19}{20}$
    (B) $\frac{4}{5}$
    (C) $\frac{11}{10}$
    (D) $\frac{1}{4}$

17. Hugo brought some pieces of candy to school. He gave $\frac{1}{3}$ of the candy to his friend Daniel, and $\frac{1}{6}$ of the candy to his teacher. If the teacher got 3 pieces of candy from Hugo, how many pieces of candy did Daniel get?

    (A)   3
    (B)   4
    (C)   5
    (D)   6

18. Which fraction is the least?

    (A) $\frac{3}{4}$

    (B) $\frac{1}{2}$

    (C) $\frac{2}{5}$

    (D) $\frac{2}{3}$

19. Which fraction is the greatest?

    (A) $\frac{4}{9}$

    (B) $\frac{50}{100}$

    (C) $\frac{4}{10}$

    (D) $\frac{11}{20}$

20. What fraction of the figure below is unshaded?

    (A) $\frac{75}{100}$

    (B) $\frac{1}{4}$

    (C) $\frac{12}{4}$

    (D) $\frac{4}{12}$

21. Which fraction is between $\frac{17}{20}$ and $\frac{19}{20}$?

    (A) $\frac{7}{10}$

    (B) $\frac{3}{5}$

    (C) $\frac{18}{40}$

    (D) $\frac{9}{10}$

22. Rafa brought some pieces of candy to school. He gave $\frac{1}{4}$ of the candy to his friend Daniel, and $\frac{1}{2}$ of the candy to his teacher. If Daniel got 10 pieces of candy from Rafa, how many pieces of candy did the teacher get?

    (A)   1

    (B)   5

    (C)   10

    (D)   20

23. Which fraction is between $\frac{70}{100}$ and $\frac{4}{5}$?

    (A) $\frac{1}{5}$

    (B) $\frac{1}{2}$

    (C) $\frac{3}{4}$

    (D) $\frac{9}{10}$

24. Which fraction is the least?

    (A) $\frac{1}{2}$

    (B) $\frac{4}{7}$

    (C) $\frac{6}{10}$

    (D) $\frac{11}{20}$

25. Which fraction is the greatest?

    (A) $\frac{1}{2}$

    (B) $\frac{16}{20}$

    (C) $\frac{3}{4}$

    (D) $\frac{7}{10}$

Estimating

Estimating questions are quite easy. The most important thing is that you pay attention to what the question asks you to round to. Is it the ones, tens, or hundreds place? Remember that you round up for numbers ending in 5 or more, and you round down for numbers ending in 4 or less.

Example #1

Jamie earns $15.24 per hour at her part-time job. Last week, she worked 4.78 hours. Which expression should she use to get the closest estimate of her pay?

(A) 15×4

(B) 20×4

(C) 15×5

(D) 20×5

Notice that this question doesn't tell you which place to round to. You need to look at all the answer choices to determine which one is the closest estimate of Jamie's pay. If you were rounding to the tens place, 15.24 would increase to 20. Two answer choices include 20. However, in this question it is more accurate to round down to 15. Therefore, the answer is either (A) or (C). 4.78 rounds up to 5, so **the correct answer is (C).**

Example #2

Apples cost $2.88 per pound and tangerines cost $4.12 per pound. Max buys 4 pounds of apples and 7 pounds of tangerines. Which expression should he use to estimate how much he paid altogether?

(A) $3 + 4 + 4 + 7$

(B) $3 \times 7 + 4 \times 4$

(C) $3 \times 4 + 4 \times 7$

(D) 7×11

This is a more advanced estimating question because it involves two parts. You can simplify it by doing things step by step. First, figure out how much Max spends on apples. 2.88 rounds up to 3, and Max bought 4 pounds of apples. To figure out the total cost, do 4×3. Tangerines cost $4.12, which you can round down to 4. Max buys 7 pounds of tangerines, so the total cost would be 4×7. Then, to find to cost of both the apples and the tangerines, add together your answers: $3 \times 4 + 4 \times 7$. **The correct answer is (C).**

Practice Problems

1. Enzo bought five packages of gum that cost $1.71 each. Which expression should he use to get the closest estimate of how much he paid?
   - (A) 5×1.0
   - (B) 5×1.5
   - (C) 5×2.0
   - (D) 5×2.5

2. Noah earns $15.95 per hour at his part-time job. Last week, he worked 12.04 hours. Which expression should he use to get the closest estimate of his pay?
   - (A) 15×12
   - (B) 16×13
   - (C) 15×13
   - (D) 16×12

3. What is 89,675 rounded to the nearest hundred?
   - (A) 89,000
   - (B) 89,600
   - (C) 89,700
   - (D) 90,000

4. Plums cost $1.92 per pound and nectarines cost $3.19 per pound. Henry buys 6 pounds of plums and 5 pounds of nectarines. Which expression should he use to estimate how much he paid altogether?
   - (A) $2 \times 6 + 3 \times 5$
   - (B) 5×11
   - (C) $2 + 6 + 3 + 5$
   - (D) $2 \times 5 + 3 \times 6$

5. What is 52 rounded to the nearest ten?
   - (A) 50
   - (B) 55
   - (C) 60
   - (D) 100

6. A warehouse stores 478 boxes, each of which contains 92 calculators. Which expression gives the best approximation of the number of calculators in the warehouse?
   - (A) 400×90
   - (B) 400×100
   - (C) 500×90
   - (D) 500×100

7. What is 449 rounded to the nearest hundred?
   - (A) 0
   - (B) 400
   - (C) 450
   - (D) 500

8. Agustin's school was collecting cans for recycling. They had 42 bags with 38 cans inside each bag. Which expression shows about how many cans they collected?
   - (A) 30×30
   - (B) 40×30
   - (C) 40×40
   - (D) 50×40

9. An airplane has 67 compartments that can hold 6 pieces of luggage each. Which expression shows about how many total pieces of luggage the airplane can hold?
   - (A) 60×10
   - (B) 70×10
   - (C) 60×5
   - (D) 70×5

10. What is 528 rounded to the nearest ten?
    - (A) 500
    - (B) 520
    - (C) 530
    - (D) 550

11. A delivery company loaded each of their 101 trucks with 61 boxes. Which expression shows approximately how many total boxes the trucks held?
    (A) 110×60
    (B) 100×60
    (C) 110×70
    (D) 100×70

12. What is 6,821 rounded to the nearest ten?
    (A)   6,800
    (B)   6,820
    (C)   6,830
    (D)   6,900

13. Stevenson was buying pencils. He bought 12 packs, and each pack had 28 pencils in it. Which expression shows about how many pencils he bought?
    (A) 10×40
    (B) 20×30
    (C) 10×30
    (D) 20×40

14. Karim works for the student newspaper, where he earns $11.15 for each article he writes and $4.95 for each photo he takes. This month, Karim wrote 3 articles and took 7 photos. Which expression should he use to estimate how much he will be paid?
    (A) 14×12
    (B) $11 + 5 + 3 + 7$
    (C) $11 \times 7 + 5 \times 3$
    (D) $11 \times 3 + 5 \times 7$

15. What is 700 rounded to the nearest ten?
    (A)   700
    (B)   710
    (C)   800
    (D)   1,000

16. Wang Su had 88 music albums on his computer. If each album was 42 minutes long, which expression shows about how many minutes of music were on Wang Su's computer?
    (A) 80×30
    (B) 90×30
    (C) 80×40
    (D) 90×40

17. Apples cost $1.99 per pound and plums cost $2.12 per pound. Max buys 2 pounds of apples and 2 pounds of plums. Which expression should he use to estimate how much he paid altogether?
    (A) $2 \times 2 \times 2 \times 2$
    (B) 4×4
    (C) $2 \times 2 + 2 \times 2$
    (D) $2 \times 2 \times 2 + 2$

18. What is 49 rounded to the nearest hundred?
    (A)   0
    (B)   40
    (C)   50
    (D)   100

19. A zoo uses 1,137 pounds of food each day to feed the animals in its exhibits. Which expression shows about how much food the zoo would use after 38 days?
    (A) $1,000 \times 35$
    (B) $1,000 \times 40$
    (C) $1,100 \times 35$
    (D) $1,100 \times 40$

20. What is 103,210 rounded to the nearest thousand?
    (A)   100,000
    (B)   103,000
    (C)   103,200
    (D)   104,000

21. What is 597 rounded to the nearest ten?
    (A)   500
    (B)   550
    (C)   590
    (D)   600

22. An industrial machine can make 89 shirts every minute. Which expression shows about how many shirts the machine will make in 52 minutes?
    (A) 85×50
    (B) 85×60
    (C) 90×50
    (D) 90×60

23. An orchard owner was counting the number of apples she had. Each of her 44 apple trees had 62 apples on it. Which expression shows about how many apples she had in total?
    (A) 45×60
    (B) 45×65
    (C) 50×60
    (D) 50×65

24. It costs $1.78 to print a small picture at a store and $5.10 to print a large picture. A student prints 9 small pictures and 15 large pictures. Which expression should he use to estimate how much he paid altogether?
    (A) 17×14
    (B) $5 \times 15 + 2 \times 9$
    (C) $2 + 9 + 5 + 15$
    (D) $2 \times 15 + 5 \times 9$

Decimals

Decimals questions on the Primary 4 ISEE will often involve shaded figures. Remember that the easiest way to find a decimal value is to create a fraction with a denominator of 100, and then move the decimal of the top number of the fraction two places to the left.

Example #1

Convert $\frac{1}{4}$ to a decimal.

(A)   0.10
(B)   0.25
(C)   0.40
(D)   0.50

You need to find a way to make the denominator of this fraction equal 100. To do this, multiply by 25. Then, since you multiplied by 25 on the bottom, you need to do the same thing on top. This results in $\frac{25}{100}$. The number on top is 25.00. Moving the decimal two places to the left results in 0.25. **The correct answer is (B).**

Example #2
What decimal represents the shaded region of the figure below?

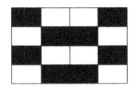

(A)   0.15
(B)   0.25
(C)   0.50
(D)   1.00

First, create a fraction. There are 16 boxes total, and 8 of the boxes are shaded, so the fraction is $\frac{8}{16}$. There is no way to make 16 multiply to 100, so you can try reducing the fraction first by dividing the top and the bottom of the fraction by 8. The fraction is equal to $\frac{1}{2}$. Now, you can multiply the top and bottom of the fraction by 50 to get $\frac{50}{100}$. The number on top of the fraction is 50.00. Move the decimal 2 places to the left to get 0.50. **The correct answer is (C).**

Example #3

A student's three dogs weigh 40.25 pounds together. Two of the dogs each weigh 14.50 pounds. What is the weight of the third dog?

(A)   10.25 pounds

(B)   11.25 pounds

(C)   22.25 pounds

(D)   25.75 pounds

This question isn't too difficult, but you must read it very carefully. The first two dogs *each* weigh 14.50 pounds, so you must do 40.25 – 14.50 – 14.50 = 11.25. **The correct answer is (B).** Make sure to line up your decimals when you subtract! (D) is a trick answer for students who only do 40.25 – 14.50.

Example #4

Josephine needs $0.50 to buy breakfast at school and $1.25 for lunch. If she went to school five days last week, how much did she spend on her meals?

(A) $1.25

(B) $7.00

(C) $8.25

(D) $10.00

First, figure out how much Josephine spends each day. Line up your decimals and add: 0.50 + 1.25 = 1.75. For older students who are more experienced with decimals, the faster way to complete the rest of this question is to do 1.75 × 5 = 8.75. **The correct answer is (C)**. However, 3rd grade students taking the ISEE are unlikely to have studied multiplying decimals in school. Therefore, we recommend that students add 1.25 + 1.25 + 1.25 + 1.25 + 1.25 = 8.25. As always, make sure to line up your decimals when you add! Notice that this question will take a while to complete, so you should leave it until you've finished all the faster, easier questions on the test.

Practice Problems

1. What decimal represents the shaded region of the figure below?

    (A)   0.10
    (B)   0.25
    (C)   0.50
    (D)   0.75

2. Which decimal represents the number of shaded circles in the figure below?

    (A)   0.10
    (B)   0.20
    (C)   0.30
    (D)   0.60

3. A student's three cats weigh 30.50 pounds together. Two of the cats each weigh 9.25 pounds. What is the weight of the third cat?
    (A)   8.50 pounds
    (B)   9.75 pounds
    (C)   12.00 pounds
    (D)   13.00 pounds

4. A student needs $0.75 to buy breakfast at school and $1.50 for lunch. If she went to school three days last week, how much did she spend on her meals?
    (A) $2.25
    (B) $6.75
    (C) $7.00
    (D) $11.25

5. Convert $\frac{1}{5}$ to a decimal.
    (A)   0.05
    (B)   0.20
    (C)   0.25
    (D)   0.50

6. Which decimal represents the number of unshaded shapes below?

    (A)   0.50
    (B)   0.70
    (C)   0.75
    (D)   1.00

7. Convert $\frac{8}{50}$ to a decimal.
    (A)   0.04
    (B)   0.08
    (C)   0.12
    (D)   0.16

8. Convert $\frac{19}{25}$ to a decimal.
    (A)   0.76
    (B)   0.77
    (C)   0.78
    (D)   0.79

9. Which decimal best represents the unshaded shapes below?

    (A)   0.20
    (B)   0.25
    (C)   0.40
    (D)   0.60

10. James needs $1.00 to buy breakfast at school and $1.75 for lunch. If he went to school five days last week, how much did he spend on his meals?
    (A) $2.75
    (B) $11.00
    (C) $12.75
    (D) $13.75

11. Jesse's three siblings weigh 225.25 pounds together. One sibling weighs 83.50 pounds, and a second sibling weighs 67.50 pounds. What is the weight of Jesse's third sibling?
    (A)   73.00 pounds
    (B)   74.25 pounds
    (C)   75.25 pounds
    (D)   149.75 pounds

12. Convert $\frac{6}{100}$ to a decimal.

   (A)   0.006
   (B)   0.060
   (C)   0.600
   (D)   6.000

13. Convert $\frac{9}{10}$ to a decimal.

   (A)   0.09
   (B)   0.18
   (C)   0.90
   (D)   9.00

14. Carol's marble collection is shown.

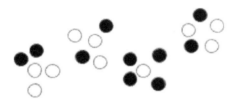

   Which decimal represents the number of black marbles in Carol's collection?

   (A)   0.10
   (B)   0.20
   (C)   0.40
   (D)   0.50

15. Small ice cream cones cost $0.75 and large ice cream cones cost $1.75. Lucille buys 3 small ice cream cones and 4 large ice cream cones for her friends. How much did she spend altogether?

   (A) $8.25
   (B) $9.25
   (C) $10.25
   (D) $11.25

16. Which decimal represents the shaded region of the figure below?

   (A)   0.40
   (B)   0.50
   (C)   0.60
   (D)   0.70

17. Convert $\frac{3}{25}$ to a decimal.

   (A)   0.03
   (B)   0.12
   (C)   0.30
   (D)   1.20

18. Which decimal represents the fraction of shaded shapes in the figure below?

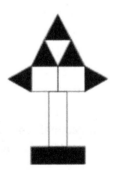

   (A)   0.60
   (B)   0.70
   (C)   0.80
   (D)   0.90

19. A student's three dogs weigh 31.50 pounds together. Two of the dogs each weigh 12.75 pounds. What is the weight of the third dog?

   (A)   6 pounds
   (B)   7 pounds
   (C)   8 pounds
   (D)   9 pounds

20. Convert $\frac{2}{4}$ to a decimal.

    (A)   0.20
    (B)   0.25
    (C)   0.50
    (D)   0.75

21. Marina's marble collection is shown.

    Which decimal represents the number of white marbles in Marina's collection?

    (A)   0.25
    (B)   0.50
    (C)   0.75
    (D)   1.00

22. What decimal represents the unshaded region of the figure below?

    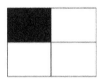

    (A)   0.25
    (B)   0.50
    (C)   0.75
    (D)   1.00

23. Convert $\frac{17}{50}$ to a decimal.

    (A)   0.17
    (B)   0.34
    (C)   0.50
    (D)   1.70

24. Convert $\frac{1}{100}$ to a decimal.

    (A)   0.0001
    (B)   0.0010
    (C)   0.0100
    (D)   0.1000

25. A student's four books weigh 19 pounds together. Two of the books each weigh 4.50 pounds. The other two books each weigh the same. What is the weight of one of the remaining books?
    (A)   2.50 pounds
    (B)   5.00 pounds
    (C)   7.50 pounds
    (D)   10.00 pounds

26. Paperback books cost $0.75 and hardcover books cost $1.50. If Greg bought 3 paperback books and 4 hardcover books, how much did he spend altogether?
    (A) $2.25
    (B) $4.50
    (C) $5.75
    (D) $8.25

27. Convert $\frac{14}{25}$ to a decimal.

    (A)   0.56
    (B)   0.60
    (C)   0.64
    (D)   0.68

Net Shapes

Net shapes test spatial reasoning abilities. That means these questions test how well you can imagine what a 3D shape looks like in your head.

Example #1
Jerome has a box shaped like a cube. He cuts some of the edges to make the box flat. Which drawing shows the flattened box?

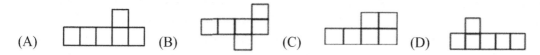

One way to practice these questions is to draw the shapes on paper, cut them out, and then see if it's possible to fold them into cubes. You should also remember that each figure must have one portion that is 4 boxes long. If there are 3 boxes or 5 boxes in a row, it is impossible to create a cube. Finally, you can memorize the following nets:

These four nets will all form cubes. Therefore, **the correct answer to the question above is (B).**

Example #2
A solid shape is shown below.

Which shows the faces of the shape?

(A)

(B)

(C)

(D)

On a question like this, it may be helpful to think about a real-life object. The shape above looks similar to a can of soup, so you should think about how many faces that can has. There is a circular bottom and top, as well as the side of can. If you unfolded the side of the can and laid it flat, it would form a rectangle, so **(B) is the correct answer**

Practice Problems

1. Malik has a box shaped like a cube. He cuts some of the edges to make the box flat. Which drawing shows the flattened box?

(A)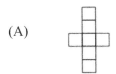

(B)

(C)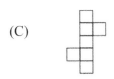

(D)

2. A solid shape is shown below.

Which shows the faces of the shape?

(A)

(B)

(C)

(D)

3. A solid shape is shown below.

Which shows the faces of the shape?

(A)

(B)

(C)

(D)

4. Aina has a box shaped like a cube. She cuts some of the edges to make the box flat. Which drawing shows the flattened box?

(A)

(B)

(C)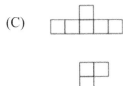

(D)

5. A solid shape is shown below.

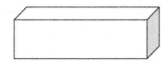

Which shows the faces of the shape?

(A)

(B)

(C)

(D)

6. Davis has a box shaped like a cube. He cuts some of the edges to make the box flat. Which drawing shows the flattened box?

(A)

(B)

(C)

(D)

7. Leon has a box shaped like a cube. He cuts some of the edges to make the box flat. Which drawing shows the flattened box?

(A)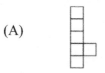

(B)

(C)

(D)

Reflections and Lines of Symmetry

Reflections and Lines of Symmetry questions ask what a shape would look like if it were reflected over a line.

Example #1
Use the figure to answer the question.

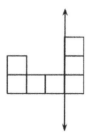

Which shows the figure after being flipped over the vertical line?

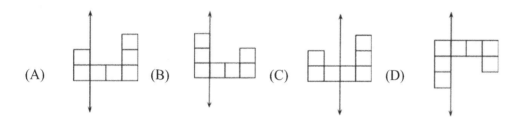

In the original figure, there are four boxes to the left of the vertical line and three boxes to the right of the vertical line. Therefore, when the figure is reflected over the vertical line, there will be three boxes to the left of the vertical line and four boxes to the right of the vertical line. You can eliminate (A). Choice (C) has simply moved the vertical line one space to the left, but the figure has not been reflected over the line. The figure in choice (D) has been flipped over the vertical line, but it has *also* been flipped upside down. Therefore, **the correct answer is (B).**

If something is *symmetrical*, that means that is has halves that are mirror images of each other. Let's look at a few examples:

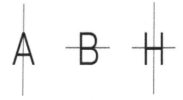

Each letter's line of symmetry has been drawn in. Notice how if you fold the letter over the line of symmetry, it will create a mirror image. *A* and *B* both have one line of symmetry, while *H* has two lines of symmetry.

Example #2

Which of the following symbols has at least one line of symmetry?

(A)   ☼

(B)   ♪

(C)   ש

(D)   ♫

(B), (C), and (D) do not contain any lines of symmetry. (A) has multiple lines of symmetry. **(A) is the correct answer.**

Practice Problems

1. Which of the following symbols contains at least one line of symmetry?

    (A)   ≈

    (B)   ▲

    (C)   ®

    (D)   ≤

2. Which of the following symbols does not have a line of symmetry?

    (A)   Ж

    (B)   Ⅲ

    (C)   Щ

    (D)   Ḣ

3. Which of the following symbols contains at least one line of symmetry?

    (A)   Ё

    (B)   ð

    (C)   ¿

    (D)   Ω

4. Which of the following symbols contains at least one line of symmetry?

    (A)   ф

    (B)   Щ

    (C)   ƀ

    (D)   j

5. Which of the following symbols does not have a line of symmetry?

    (A)   Ï

    (B)   ☼

    (C)   ☺

    (D)   ₡

6. Which of the following symbols does not have a line of symmetry?

    (A)   ♥

    (B)   ✕

    (C)   ℮

    (D)   ÷

7. Use the figure to answer the question.

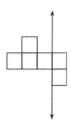

Which shows the figure after being flipped over the vertical line?

(A)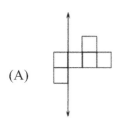

(B)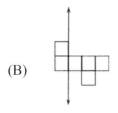

(C)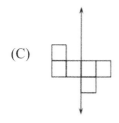

(D)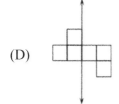

8. Use the figure to answer the question.

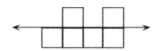

Which shows the figure after being flipped over the horizontal line?

(A)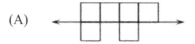

(B)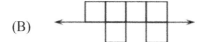

(C)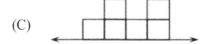

(D)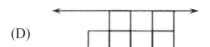

9. Use the figure to answer the question.

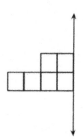

Which shows the figure after being flipped over the vertical line?

(A)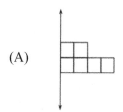

(B)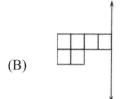

(C)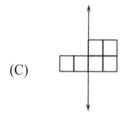

(D)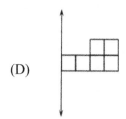

10. Use the figure to answer the question.

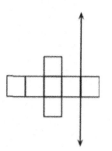

Which shows the figure after being flipped over the vertical line?

(A)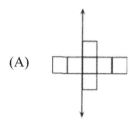

(B)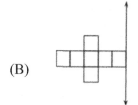

(C)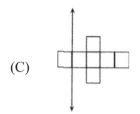

(D)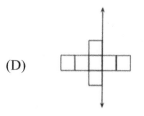

11. Use the figure to answer the question.

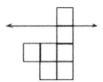

Which shows the figure after being flipped over the horizontal line?

(A)

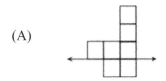

(B)

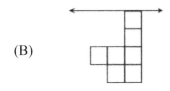

(C)

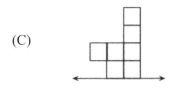

(D)

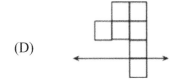

12. Which of the following letters contains at least one line of symmetry?

(A)   I

(B)   J

(C)   P

(D)   Q

13. Which of the following letters contains at least one line of symmetry?

(A)   Z

(B)   O

(C)   N

(D)   G

14. Which of the following letters does not contain a line of symmetry?

(A)   O

(B)   E

(C)   T

(D)   R

Coordinate Grids

If you know the fundamentals of *coordinate grids*, these questions will be very easy.

Example #1
Which point is located at (5,4) on the coordinate grid below?

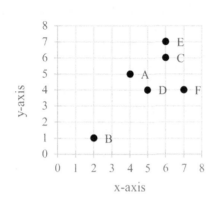

(A)   *A*
(B)   *B*
(C)   *C*
(D)   *D*

The given point is (5,4). Start at (0,0) and move 5 spaces to the right. Then, move 4 spaces up. You land on point *D*, so **(D) is the correct answer.**

Example #2
Sergei draws a path on the coordinate grid. He begins at point (3,3) and moves 2 spaces right and 3 spaces up.

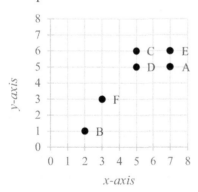

What is the point where Sergei lands?
(A)   *A*
(B)   *B*
(C)   *C*
(D)   *D*

Start at the origin and move 3 spaces right and 3 spaces up to land on point *F*: this is your starting point. From there, move 2 spaces right and 3 spaces up to land on point *C*. **(C) is the correct answer.**

Example #3

Use the coordinate grid to answer the question.

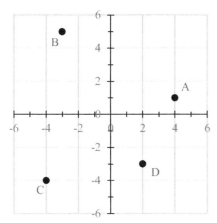

Which of the points on the graph is closest to (4,-2)?

(A)   A
(B)   B
(C)   C
(D)   D

First, identify the point (4,-2) on the graph. It is in between Point *A* and Point *D*, but it falls closer to Point *D*. Therefore, **(D) is the correct answer.**

Practice Problems

1. Aisha draws a path on the coordinate grid. She begins at point (3,1) and moves 2 spaces right and 3 spaces up.

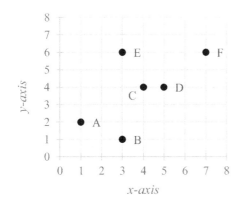

What is the point where Aisha lands?

(A)   *C*
(B)   *D*
(C)   *E*
(D)   *F*

2. What are the coordinates of Point *C* below?

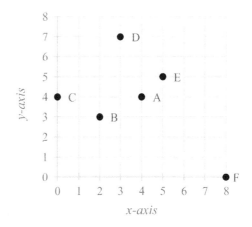

(A)   (2,3)
(B)   (3,2)
(C)   (0,4)
(D)   (4,0)

3. Which point is located at (0,4) on the coordinate grid below?

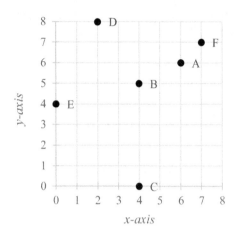

(A)   *B*
(B)   *C*
(C)   *D*
(D)   *E*

4. Ivan draws a path on the coordinate grid. He begins at point (0,1) and moves 4 spaces right and 2 spaces up.

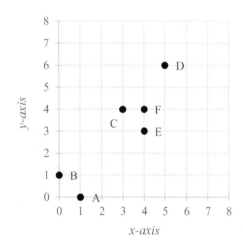

What is the point where Ivan lands?
(A)   *C*
(B)   *D*
(C)   *E*
(D)   *F*

5. Konstantinos draws a path on the coordinate grid. He begins at point (3,0) and moves 2 spaces right and 5 spaces up.

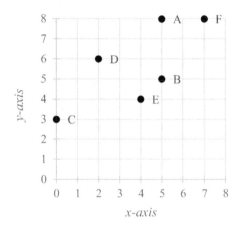

What is the point where Konstantinos lands?
(A)   *A*
(B)   *B*
(C)   *C*
(D)   *D*

6. What are the coordinates of Point *B* below?

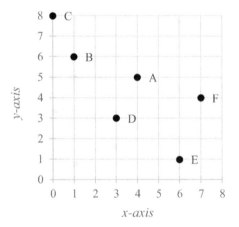

(A)   (1,6)
(B)   (3,3)
(C)   (6,1)
(D)   (0,8)

7. Lina draws a path on the coordinate
    grid. She begins at point (2,4) and
    moves 1 space right and 1 space up.

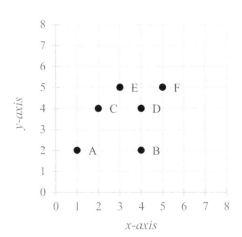

What is the point where Lina lands?
(A)   B
(B)   C
(C)   D
(D)   E

8. What are the coordinates of Point E
    below?

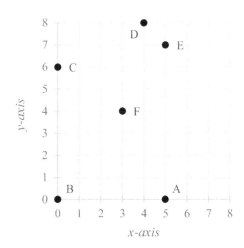

(A)   (0,0)
(B)   (4,4)
(C)   (5,0)
(D)   (5,7)

9. Which point is located at (3,4) on the
    coordinate grid below?

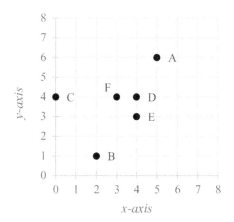

(A)   C
(B)   D
(C)   E
(D)   F

10. Ari draws a path on the coordinate grid.
    He begins at point (1,2) and moves 6
    spaces right and 3 spaces up.

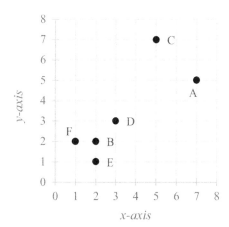

What is the point where Ari lands?
(A)   A
(B)   B
(C)   C
(D)   D

11. Martina draws a path on the coordinate grid. She begins at point (3,1) and moves 2 spaces right and 3 spaces up.

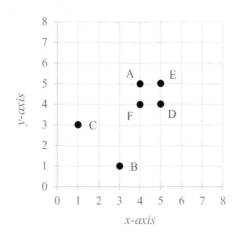

What is the point where Martina lands?
(A)   A
(B)   B
(C)   C
(D)   D

12. Use the coordinate grid to answer the question.

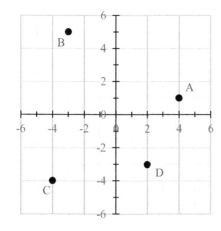

Which of the points on the graph is closest to (-3,3)?
(A)   A
(B)   B
(C)   C
(D)   D

13. Use the coordinate grid to answer the question.

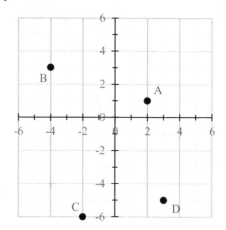

Which of the points on the graph is closest to (2,-4)?
(A)   A
(B)   B
(C)   C
(D)   D

14. Use the coordinate grid to answer the question.

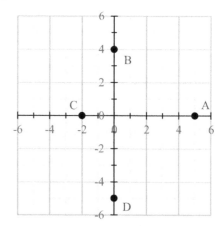

Which of the points on the graph is closest to (0,0)?
(A)   A
(B)   B
(C)   C
(D)   D

15. Use the coordinate grid to answer the question.

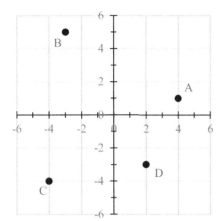

Which of the points on the graph is closest to (0,6)?

(A)   *A*
(B)   *B*
(C)   *C*
(D)   *D*

16. Use the coordinate grid to answer the question.

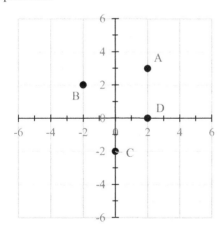

Which of the points on the graph is closest to (1,2)?

(A)   *A*
(B)   *B*
(C)   *C*
(D)   *D*

17. Use the coordinate grid to answer the question.

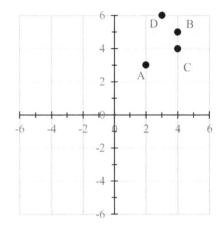

Which of the points on the graph is closest to (6,4)?

(A)   *A*
(B)   *B*
(C)   *C*
(D)   *D*

18. Use the coordinate grid to answer the question.

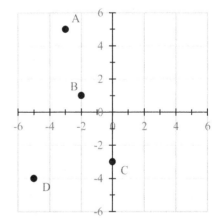

Which of the points on the graph is closest to (-4,-3)?

(A)   *A*
(B)   *B*
(C)   *C*
(D)   *D*

Clue Tables

Clue tables use symbols to test your knowledge of the order of operations.

Example #1

Meredith solves a problem using the clue table.

Clue Table

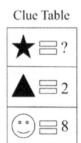

In the equation ☺ + (▲ × ★) = 16, what is the value of ★?

(A)   1
(B)   2
(C)   3
(D)   4

Make sure to think about PEMDAS. The first step is to plug in the numbers you do know. ▲ = 2, and ☺ = 8, so you can rewrite the equation as 8 + (2 × ★) = 16.

Do you remember the Working Backwards strategy from Part II? It works extremely well for these questions. Try plugging in 2 for ★. 8 + (2 × 2) = 12. This answer is too small, so try (D).

8 + (2 × 4) = 8 + 8 = 16. **(D) is the correct answer.**

Practice Problems

1. Omolo solves a problem using the clue table.

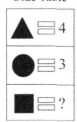

Clue Table

In the equation $(2 + \blacktriangle) \times \blacksquare = 36$, what is the value of $\blacksquare$?

(A)   3
(B)   4
(C)   5
(D)   6

2. Hamza solves a problem using the clue table.

Clue Table

In the equation $3 \times (\blacktriangle + \blacksquare) = 21$, what is the value of $\blacksquare$?

(A)   3
(B)   4
(C)   5
(D)   6

3. Rita solves a problem using the clue table.

Clue Table

In the equation $\blacksquare \times \bullet \times 2 = 42$, what is the value of $\bullet$?

(A)   3
(B)   4
(C)   5
(D)   6

4. Kevin solves a problem using the clue table.

Clue Table

In the equation $2 \times (\bigstar + \blacktriangle) = 12$, what is the value of $\blacktriangle$?

(A)   1
(B)   2
(C)   3
(D)   4

5. Agustin solves a problem using the clue table.

Clue Table

In the equation ☺ + (▲ × ★) = 16, what is the value of ★?

(A)   1
(B)   2
(C)   3
(D)   4

6. Wilson solves a problem using the clue table.

Clue Table

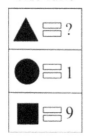

In the equation (▲ × ●) + (■ × ●) = 14, what is the value of ▲?

(A)   2
(B)   3
(C)   4
(D)   5

7. Mason solves a problem using the clue table.

Clue Table

If (▲ × ☺) + (☺ × ★) = 40, what is the value of ★?

(A)   1
(B)   2
(C)   3
(D)   4

8. Zoe solves a problem using the clue table.

Clue Table

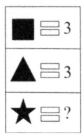

If (▲ × ■) + (5 × ★) = 34, what is the value of ★?

(A)   5
(B)   6
(C)   7
(D)   8

Charts

The Primary 4 ISEE has some *charts* questions that are unique to this test.

Example #1

An ice cream man counted the number of ice cream cones he sold each day for 5 days. He sold 24 more cones on Thursday and Friday combined than he did on Monday.

ICE CREAM CONES SOLD PER DAY

Monday	🍦 🍦 🍦
Tuesday	🍦
Wednesday	🍦 🍦 🍦 🍦 🍦 🍦
Thursday	🍦 🍦 🍦
Friday	🍦 🍦 🍦 🍦

Based on the data, how many ice cream cones are represented by the 🍦 ?

(A)   4
(B)   5
(C)   6
(D)   7

The best way to answer these questions is by working backwards. If (A) is correct, the ice cream man sold 28 cones on Thursday and Friday combined (because 3 + 4 = 7, and 7 × 4 = 28) and 12 cones on Monday. 28 – 12 = 16, but the question says he sold 24 more cones on Thursday and Friday combined, so this answer is incorrect. Let's jump to (C). If (C) is correct, the ice cream man sold 42 cones on Thursday and Friday combined (because 3 + 4 = 7, and 7 × 6 = 42) and 18 cones on Monday. 42 – 18 = 24, so **(C) is the correct answer**.

If you don't want to work backwards, you should first find how many cones the ice cream man sold on Thursday and Friday combined. Based on the chart, there are 7 cones. On Monday, he sold 3 cones. 7 – 3 = 4, so there is a difference of 4 cones. Then, ask yourself "4 times what equals 24?" 4 × 6 = 24, so you know (C) is the correct answer.

Example #2

The chart shows the number of ice cream cones sold by an ice cream man per day.
(🍦 = 4 ice cream cones)

ICE CREAM CONES SOLD PER DAY

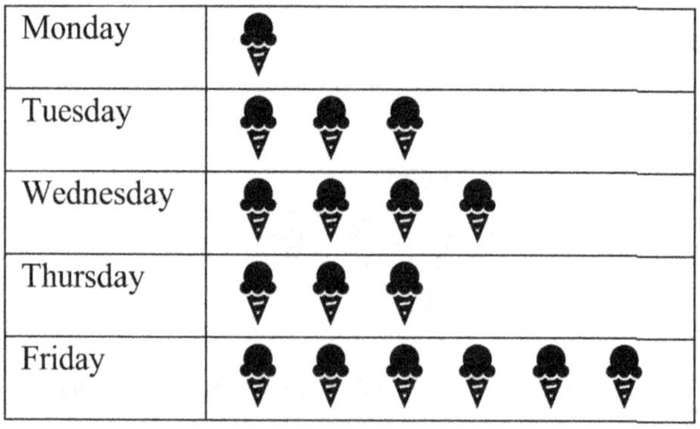

Monday	🍦
Tuesday	🍦 🍦 🍦
Wednesday	🍦 🍦 🍦 🍦
Thursday	🍦 🍦 🍦
Friday	🍦 🍦 🍦 🍦 🍦 🍦

What is the total number of ice cream cones sold on Wednesday and Friday combined?

(A)   10
(B)   24
(C)   40
(D)   48

This is an easier version of Example #1. Instead of figuring out how many actual ice cream cones each icon represents, you just have to add up the 4 cones sold on Wednesday and the 6 cones sold on Friday and multiply by 4. 6 + 4 = 10, and 10 × 4 = 40. **The correct answer is (C).** (A) is a trick answer for students who forget to multiply by 4.

Mathematics Question Types

Practice Problems

1. Dan recorded the number of toy dinosaurs he had in five different toy boxes. He counted 4 more toy dinosaurs in boxes 3, 4, and 5 combined than he did in box 2.

DINOSAURS PER TOY BOX

Box 1	
Box 2	
Box 3	
Box 4	
Box 5	

Based on the data, how many toy dinosaurs are represented by the ?
(A)   1
(B)   2
(C)   3
(D)   4

---

2. The chart shows the number of pieces of sushi eaten by five different students at lunch. (= 3 pieces of sushi)

PIECES OF SUSHI EATEN

Student 1	
Student 2	
Student 3	
Student 4	
Student 5	

What is the total number of pieces of sushi eaten by students 1, 2, and 4?
(A)   24
(B)   27
(C)   30
(D)   33

3. The chart shows the number of students in five classrooms who play the piano. (🎹 = 6 students)

PIANISTS PER CLASSROOM

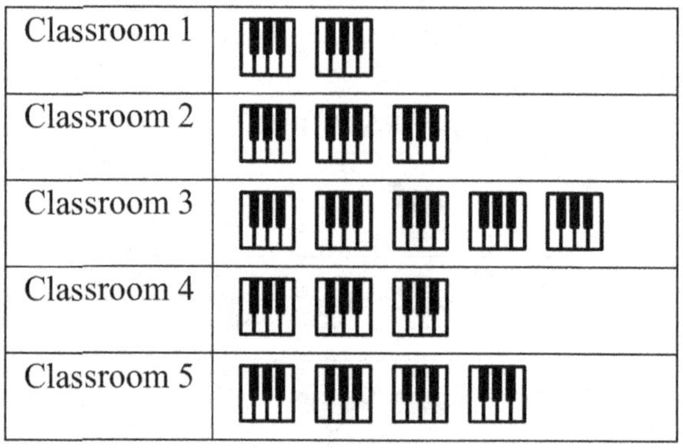

Classroom 1	🎹 🎹
Classroom 2	🎹 🎹 🎹
Classroom 3	🎹 🎹 🎹 🎹 🎹
Classroom 4	🎹 🎹 🎹
Classroom 5	🎹 🎹 🎹 🎹

What is the total number of students in classrooms 1 and 4 who play piano?

(A)　12
(B)　18
(C)　24
(D)　30

4. Rasmus recorded the number of hummingbirds at the feeder each day for five days. He spotted 3 more hummingbirds on Friday than he did on Monday and Thursday combined.

HUMMINGBIRDS SPOTTED EACH DAY

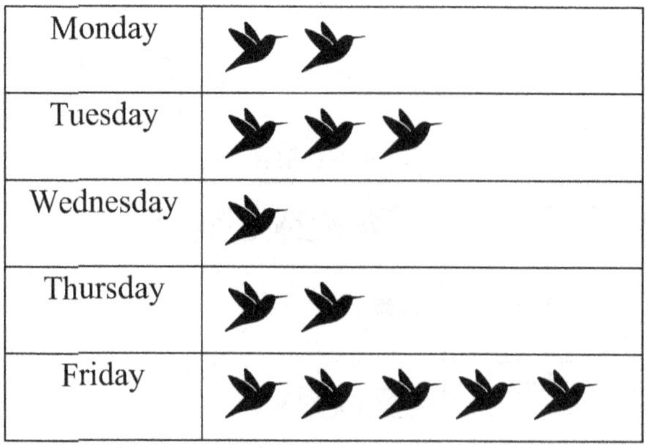

Monday	🐦 🐦
Tuesday	🐦 🐦 🐦
Wednesday	🐦
Thursday	🐦 🐦
Friday	🐦 🐦 🐦 🐦 🐦

Based on the data, how many hummingbirds are represented by the 🐦?

(A)　1
(B)　3
(C)　5
(D)　7

5. Emil recorded the number of ladybugs on a plant each day for five days. He spotted 16 more ladybugs on Thursday than he did on Wednesday.

LADYBUGS SPOTTED EACH DAY

Monday	🐞 🐞 🐞
Tuesday	🐞 🐞 🐞 🐞 🐞
Wednesday	🐞 🐞
Thursday	🐞 🐞 🐞 🐞 🐞 🐞
Friday	🐞 🐞 🐞

Based on the data, how many ladybugs are represented by the 🐞 ?

(A)   2
(B)   4
(C)   6
(D)   8

6. Lucy recorded the number of beakers in each of the 5 science labs at her high school. There were 15 more beakers in Room 5 than there were in Rooms 3 and 4 combined.

BEAKERS PER CLASSROOM

Room 1	⚗ ⚗
Room 2	⚗ ⚗ ⚗ ⚗
Room 3	⚗
Room 4	⚗
Room 5	⚗ ⚗ ⚗ ⚗ ⚗

Based on the data, how many beakers are represented by the ⚗ ?

(A)   1
(B)   3
(C)   5
(D)   7

7.   The chart shows the number of dinosaur fossils found at five different archeological sites.
     (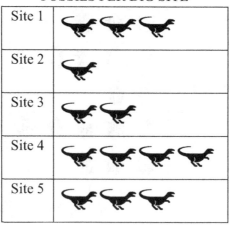 = 12 fossils)

FOSSILS PER DIG SITE

Site 1	🦖 🦖 🦖
Site 2	🦖
Site 3	🦖 🦖
Site 4	🦖 🦖 🦖 🦖
Site 5	🦖 🦖 🦖

What is the total number of fossils found at dig sites 3 and 5?
(A)   60
(B)   72
(C)   84
(D)   96

8.   Teresa surveyed the students in 5 classrooms. She asked how many students per room took piano lessons. There were 9 more piano students in Rooms 2 and 4 combined than there were in Rooms 1 and 3 combined.

PIANISTS PER CLASSROOM

Classroom 1	🎹 🎹
Classroom 2	🎹 🎹 🎹
Classroom 3	🎹
Classroom 4	🎹 🎹 🎹
Classroom 5	🎹 🎹 🎹 🎹 🎹

Based on the data, how many piano students are represented by the 🎹 ?
(A)   1
(B)   3
(C)   5
(D)   7

154

9. Pippa recorded the number of lions she saw on a 5 day safari. She spotted 20 more lions on Tuesday than she did on Wednesday and Thursday combined.

LIONS SPOTTED EACH DAY

Monday	🦁🦁🦁🦁
Tuesday	🦁🦁🦁🦁🦁🦁
Wednesday	🦁
Thursday	🦁🦁
Friday	🦁🦁🦁

Based on the data, how many lions are represented by the 🦁 ?

(A)   2
(B)   5
(C)   10
(D)   20

10. Cesar recorded the number of pieces of sushi 5 different students ate at lunch. Students 2 and 4 combined ate 25 more pieces of sushi than students 1 and 3 combined.

PIECES OF SUSHI EATEN

Student 1	🍣🍣
Student 2	🍣🍣🍣
Student 3	🍣
Student 4	🍣🍣🍣🍣🍣
Student 5	🍣🍣

Based on the data, how many pieces of sushi are represented by the 🍣 ?

(A)   1
(B)   3
(C)   5
(D)   7

Symbols

Symbol questions test you on basic arithmetic, but they are slightly more difficult than simple addition, subtraction, multiplication, and division questions because they involve the use of unusual symbols.

Example #1

If ♥ × 2 + 4 = 16, what number does ♥ stand for?

(A)   4
(B)   5
(C)   6
(D)   7

Working backwards is a great strategy for these questions. You'll need to remember your order of operations, or PEMDAS: first, you'll multiply the number by 2, and then you'll add 4 to that product. The final result is 16. Let's try (B). 5 × 2 + 4 = 10 + 4 = 14. This answer is too small, so try (C). 6 × 2 + 4 = 12 + 4 = 16. **(C) is the correct answer.**

Example #2

These symbols have the following meaning:

▶ = multiply ☼ = 3 ◊ = 6 ♦ = add

What is the value of 16 ♦ ☼ ▶ ◊ = ?

(A)   24
(B)   34
(C)   104
(D)   114

These questions are a bit more difficult. First, you should rewrite the equation on a piece of paper, replace the symbols with the correct operation or number, and solve.

16 ♦ ☼ ▶ ◊ = 16 (add) (3) (multiply) (6) = 16 + 3 × 6 = 16 + 18 = 34

The correct answer is (B). (D) is a trick answer. If you forget PEMDAS and do the math from left to right, you'll get 16 + 3 × 6 = 19 × 6 = 114. Don't make this careless mistake!

Practice Problems

1. If ♥ × 3 + 7 = 10, what number does ♥ stand for?
   (A)   0
   (B)   1
   (C)   2
   (D)   3

2. These symbols have the following meaning:

   ◊ = multiply ☺ = 7 ▶ = 6 ♦ = divide

   What is the value of 35 ♦ ☺ ◊ ▶ = ?
   (A)   25
   (B)   30
   (C)   35
   (D)   40

3. These symbols have the following meaning:

   ♥ = multiply ☺ = 3 ♦ = 6 ◊ = add

   What is the value of 5 ♥ ♦ ◊ ☺ = ?
   (A)   25
   (B)   28
   (C)   33
   (D)   45

4. If 15 ÷ ♥ + 5 = 10, what number does ♥ stand for?
   (A)   3
   (B)   4
   (C)   5
   (D)   6

5. If ♦ + 2 × 5 = 20, what number does ♦ stand for?
   (A)   2
   (B)   4
   (C)   7
   (D)   10

6. These symbols have the following meaning:

   ▶ = multiply ☼ = 5 ◊ = 3 ♦ = add

   What is the value of 5 ♦ ☼ ▶ ◊ = ?
   (A)   20
   (B)   30
   (C)   50
   (D)   75

7. If 4 + 4 × ☺ = 16, what number does ☺ stand for?
   (A)   2
   (B)   3
   (C)   4
   (D)   5

8. If ▶ ÷ 7 + 3 = 9, what number does ▶ stand for?
   (A)   6
   (B)   7
   (C)   42
   (D)   90

9. If ▶ × ▶ + 7 = 32, what number does ▶ stand for?
   (A)   3
   (B)   4
   (C)   5
   (D)   6

10. These symbols have the following meaning:

    ▶ = divide ♥ = 8 ◊ = 5 ☺ = add

    What is the value of 16 ▶ ♥ ☺ ◊ = ?
    (A)   4
    (B)   5
    (C)   6
    (D)   7

11. If ☺ × 3 + ☺ = 4, what number does ☺ stand for?
    (A)   1
    (B)   2
    (C)   3
    (D)   4

12. These symbols have the following meaning:

    ► = divide ☼ = 12 ◊ = 4 ♦ = add

    What is the value of 16 ♦ ☼ ► ◊ = ?
    (A)   19
    (B)   20
    (C)   21
    (D)   22

13. These symbols have the following meaning:

    ☺ = multiply ☼ = 3 ◊ = 6 ♥ = add

    What is the value of 6 ♥ ◊ ☺ ☼ = ?
    (A)   24
    (B)   28
    (C)   32
    (D)   36

14. These symbols have the following meaning:

    ► = multiply ☼ = 4 ◊ = 2 ♦ = add

    What is the value of 3 ♦ ☼ ► ◊ = ?
    (A)   11
    (B)   12
    (C)   13
    (D)   14

15. If ♦ × ♦ × ♦ − 3 = 24, what number does ♦ stand for?
    (A)   2
    (B)   3
    (C)   4
    (D)   5

16. These symbols have the following meaning:

    ► = multiply ☼ = 3 ◊ = 6 ♦ = divide

    What is the value of 24 ♦ ☼ ► ◊ = ?
    (A)   48
    (B)   50
    (C)   52
    (D)   54

17. If ♥ × 2 − 4 = 12, what number does ♥ stand for?
    (A)   5
    (B)   6
    (C)   7
    (D)   8

18. If ► ÷ 5 − 6 = 4, what number does ► stand for?
    (A)   45
    (B)   50
    (C)   55
    (D)   60

19. These symbols have the following meaning:

    ► = multiply ☼ = 5 ◊ = 8 ♦ = divide

    What is the value of 40 ♦ ☼ ► ◊ = ?
    (A)   1
    (B)   60
    (C)   64
    (D)   72

Currency

Currency questions involve multiple steps and a lot of decimals. It's important to read the directions carefully to make sure you don't make any careless mistakes!

Example #1

A girl had $5.44 in her purse. On her way to the beach, she found a five-dollar bill, two quarters, and seven nickels. How much money does she have now?

(A) $11.09
(B) $11.19
(C) $11.29
(D) $11.39

The girl starts with $5.44. A five-dollar bill = $5.00, two quarters = $0.50, and seven nickels = $0.35. Add everything together: $5.44 + $5.00 + $0.50 + $0.35 = $11.29. **(C) is the correct answer.**

Example #2

A boy has 17 quarters, 7 dimes, 6 nickels, and 15 pennies in a jar. If he spends $1.75 on lunch, how much money will he have left?

(A) $3.65
(B) $4.55
(C) $5.40
(D) $6.20

First, find out how much money is in the jar. There are four quarters in a dollar, eight quarters in two dollars, twelve quarters in three dollars, and sixteen quarters in four dollars. That means the boy has four dollars + 1 quarter = $4.25 in quarters. 7 dimes = $0.70, 6 nickels = $0.30, and 15 pennies = $0.15. $4.25 + $0.70 + $0.30 + $0.15 = $5.40. Then, subtract $1.75 from $5.40 to get $3.65. **The correct answer is (A).** Remember to stack your numbers and line up the decimals when you're adding and subtracting!

Notice how long this question takes to do. If you see a question like this on the real test, you should do all the other questions first and come back to this one only if you have time remaining.

Practice Problems

1. A girl had $14.32 in her purse. On her way to the movies, she found a ten-dollar bill and five nickels. How much money does she have now?
    - (A) $24.32
    - (B) $24.37
    - (C) $24.57
    - (D) $24.82

2. A boy has 14 quarters, 10 dimes, 5 nickels, and 13 pennies in a jar. If he spends $2.50 on lunch, how much money will he have left?
    - (A) $2.38
    - (B) $2.58
    - (C) $3.88
    - (D) $7.38

3. A music store is having a holiday sale. The store will give $10.00 off the second item a customer purchases. Billy buys a TV for $120.00 and a CD for $14.50. How much does he pay in total?
    - (A) $112.50
    - (B) $116.50
    - (C) $120.50
    - (D) $124.50

4. A girl has 7 quarters, 5 dimes, 12 nickels, and 5 pennies in a jar. If she spends $0.75 on a candy bar, how much money will she have left?
    - (A) $2.05
    - (B) $2.10
    - (C) $2.15
    - (D) $2.90

5. A boy had $20.02 in his wallet. On his way to the store, he found a five-dollar bill, six dimes, and twenty pennies. How much money does he have now?
    - (A) $25.52
    - (B) $25.82
    - (C) $25.83
    - (D) $25.92

6. Melinda has 15 quarters, 7 dimes, 2 nickels, and 42 pennies in a jar. If she spends $4.00 on lunch, how much money will she have left?
    - (A) $0.97
    - (B) $1.97
    - (C) $2.97
    - (D) $8.97

7. A boy has 10 quarters, 10 dimes, 10 nickels, and 10 pennies in a jar. If he spends $1.35 on a snack, how much money will he have left?
    - (A) $2.75
    - (B) $2.85
    - (C) $2.95
    - (D) $3.05

8. Mr. Clark was given some change at the grocery store. He was given 3 one-dollar bills, 4 quarters, 5 dimes, and 7 pennies. How much change did he get?
    - (A) $4.27
    - (B) $4.32
    - (C) $4.45
    - (D) $4.57

9. A girl had $24.14 in her purse. On her way to a friend's house, she found four one-dollar bills, three quarters, and five dimes. How much money does she have now?
   - (A) $29.14
   - (B) $29.25
   - (C) $29.39
   - (D) $29.42

10. Mr. Thomas has $32.50. At the store, he bought 3 cookies that cost $1.50 each. How much money does he have left?
    - (A) $26.50
    - (B) $28.00
    - (C) $31.00
    - (D) $34.00

11. Dennis has 9 quarters, 2 dimes, 21 nickels, and 24 pennies in a jar. If he spends $1.25 on an ice cream cone, how much money will he have left?
    - (A) $2.25
    - (B) $2.49
    - (C) $3.12
    - (D) $3.74

12. Jasmine had $8.19 in her purse. On her way to the store, she found a twenty-dollar bill, five pennies, two dimes, and one quarter. How much money does she have now?
    - (A) $28.69
    - (B) $28.79
    - (C) $28.89
    - (D) $28.99

13. Jeff has $45.00. At the store, he bought 4 sandwiches that cost $6.00 each. How much money does he have left?
    - (A) $18.00
    - (B) $19.00
    - (C) $20.00
    - (D) $21.00

14. Jeremy had $25.25 in his wallet. On his way to school, he found a one-dollar bill, twelve dimes, and thirteen pennies. How much money does he have now?
    - (A) $27.56
    - (B) $27.57
    - (C) $27.58
    - (D) $27.59

15. A woman has $52.00 At the store, she bought 5 apples that cost $2.00 each. How much money does she have left?
    - (A) $39.00
    - (B) $40.00
    - (C) $41.00
    - (D) $42.00

16. A restaurant is offering a special deal: customers receive $7.50 off the second item they order at their meal. Two friends order a hamburger that costs $12.25 and a steak that costs $25.75. How much do they pay in total?
    - (A) $23.00
    - (B) $30.50
    - (C) $34.50
    - (D) $38.00

17. A student buys 3 notebooks for $1.20 each, a box of pencils for $1.50, and a box of pens for $1.80. How much did the student spend all together?
    - (A) $4.50
    - (B) $6.90
    - (C) $7.10
    - (D) $7.20

18. A woman has $57.75. At the store, she bought 4 donuts that cost $1.25 each. How much money does she have left?
    - (A) $50.25
    - (B) $51.50
    - (C) $52.75
    - (D) $55.25

Math Stories

Math stories ask you to translate English into math or vice versa. They are often multi-step questions that test your knowledge of addition, subtraction, multiplication, and division.

Example #1
Jonas begins the day with 389 beads in his collection. After making four bracelets, he has 149 beads remaining in his collection. Assuming he used the same number of beads for each bracelet, how many beads must he have used for each bracelet?

(A)   60
(B)   80
(C)   220
(D)   240

First, you need to find how many beads Jonas used to make all four bracelets. To do this, subtract 149 from 389 to get 240. That means Jonas used 240 beads to make all 4 bracelets. To determine how many beads he used on each individual bracelet, you must divide 240 by 4, which results in 60. **The correct answer is (A).**

Example #2
Which story best fits the equation $3 \times 9 = 27$?

(A)   I have 27 cookies. After eating 3 cookies, how many cookies do I have left?
(B)   I want to share 27 cookies with 9 friends. How many cookies do they each get?
(C)   I have 3 boxes of cookies, with 9 cookies in each box. How many cookies do I have altogether?
(D)   I have 3 boxes of cookies, and my friend has 9 boxes of cookies. How many boxes of cookies do we have altogether?

On these questions, the four answer choices will usually include an option for addition, subtraction, multiplication, and division. Here, (A) represents subtraction. If you were to rewrite this answer choice, it would be $27 - 3 = 24$. (B) represents division; it would be rewritten as $27 \div 9 = 3$. (C) represents multiplication and would be rewritten as $3 \times 9 = 27$. (D) represents addition, and would be rewritten as $3 + 9 = 12$. **(C) is the correct answer.**

Practice Problems

1. Which story best fits the equation $4 \times 6 = 24$?

    (A)   I have 24 cookies. After eating 6 cookies, how many cookies do I have left?

    (B)   I want to share 24 cookies with 6 friends. How many cookies do we each get?

    (C)   I have 4 boxes of cookies, with 6 cookies in each box. How many cookies do I have altogether?

    (D)   I have 6 boxes of cookies, and my friend has 4 boxes of cookies. How many boxes of cookies do we have altogether?

2. Jeramiah bought 78 tickets at the state fair. He spent 13 tickets on snacks, and he used the rest on rides. If each ride cost 5 tickets, how many rides could Jeramiah go on?

    (A)   13
    (B)   14
    (C)   15
    (D)   16

3. There are 6 rows of apps with 6 apps in each row on the home screen of Tom's tablet. If Tom deleted 8 apps, how many would there be remaining on his home screen?

    (A)   25
    (B)   26
    (C)   27
    (D)   28

4. A baker made 6 batches of chocolate chip cookies. Each batch contained 18 cookies. Then, the baker made an additional 13 sugar cookies. How many cookies did he bake in total?

    (A)   108
    (B)   121
    (C)   128
    (D)   135

5. Which story best fits the equation $100 \div 10 = 10$?

    (A)   I have 100 pencils, and I give 10 pencils to my friend. How many pencils do I have remaining?

    (B)   I have 10 boxes of pencils, and each box has 10 pencils in it. How many pencils do I have?

    (C)   I have 100 pencils, and my friend gives me 10 more pencils. How many pencils do I have now?

    (D)   I want to share 100 pencils evenly with 10 friends. How many pencils do they each get?

6. A donation center filled up 8 small bins with canned food. Each of the bins contained 9 cans of food. The center plans to send all the cans to 6 different families, and they want to give the same number of cans to each family. How many cans should they send to each of the 6 families?

    (A)   8
    (B)   9
    (C)   12
    (D)   66

7. A student has 14 crayons, and she decides to buy 5 more boxes of crayons. Each box has 23 crayons in it. How many crayons does the student have after she buys the 5 boxes?

(A)   42
(B)   115
(C)   129
(D)   137

8. Tiffany begins the day with 512 beads in her collection. After making five bracelets, she has 387 beads remaining in her collection. Assuming she used the same number of beads for each bracelet, how many beads must she have used for each bracelet?

(A)   15
(B)   25
(C)   100
(D)   125

9. Which story best fits the equation $2 \times 15 = 30$?

(A)   A homework assignment is 2 pages, and there are 15 questions on each page. How many questions are there altogether?

(B)   One teacher gives a student 2 homework questions, and another teacher gives the same student 15 homework questions. How many questions does the student have to do?

(C)   A student completes 15 homework questions out of 30 total questions. How many questions remain?

(D)   A student has 30 homework questions. The student's friend helps him complete 2 questions. How many questions remain?

10. There are 103 students trying out for the school's math teams. If 33 students are not picked for the teams, and the remaining students are equally divided onto 10 different teams, how many students will there be on each team?

(A)   6
(B)   7
(C)   8
(D)   9

11. Which story best fits the equation $24 \div 4 = 6$?

(A)   I have 24 stuffed animals, and I put the stuffed animals into groups of 4 and place them in boxes. How many boxes do I have?

(B)   I have 24 boxes of stuffed animals, and each box has 4 animals in it. How many total stuffed animals do I have?

(C)   I have 24 stuffed animals, and I give away 4. How many stuffed animals do I have remaining?

(D)   I want to share 24 stuffed animals equally with 6 friends. How many stuffed animals do they each get?

12. At dinner, a waiter had 22 customers, and 7 of them did not leave a tip. If the waiter got $12 from each of the customers who did leave a tip, how much money did the waiter earn in tips?

(A) $150
(B) $160
(C) $170
(D) $180

13. A chef bought 9 bags of apples for $45 dollars. Each bag had 6 apples, but the chef had to throw away 12 rotten apples. How many apples remained after the chef threw out the rotten apples?
    (A)   28
    (B)   36
    (C)   42
    (D)   52

14. A student baked 109 cupcakes for her school's bake sale. If her brother ate 17 of the cupcakes, how many packages of cupcakes could the student make if she put 2 cupcakes in each package?
    (A)   23
    (B)   46
    (C)   90
    (D)   92

15. Which story best fits the equation $5 \times 5 = 25$?

    (A)   I have 5 coffee cups, and my friend gives me 5 more. How many total coffee cups do I have now?
    (B)   Each of my 5 friends has 5 coffee cups. How many total coffee cups do my friends have?
    (C)   I have 25 coffee cups, and I want to give an equal number of coffee cups to each of my 5 friends. How many coffee cups does each friend get?
    (D)   I have 25 coffee cups, and I give away 5 of them. How many coffee cups do I have left?

16. A student has a collection of 134 books. After buying 26 more books, the student organizes the books onto 8 bookshelves. If each bookshelf holds the same number of books, how many books are there on each bookshelf?
    (A)   5
    (B)   10
    (C)   15
    (D)   20

17. Which story best fits the equation $8 - 6 = 2$?

    (A)   The tiger enclosure at a zoo has 8 tigers. The zoo gives 6 tigers to another zoo. How many tigers remain?
    (B)   A zoo has 8 tiger enclosures, and each enclosure has 2 tigers in it. How many total tigers does the zoo have?
    (C)   A zoo has 8 tigers and wants to put an equal number of tigers into 2 enclosures. How many tigers are placed in each enclosure?
    (D)   A zoo has 2 tigers, and another zoo gives this zoo 6 more tigers. How many total tigers does the zoo have now?

18. A student begins the day with 1,125 beads in his collection. After making seven bracelets, the student has 635 beads remaining in his collection. Assuming he used the same number of beads for each bracelet, how many beads must he have used for each bracelet?
    (A)   7
    (B)   35
    (C)   60
    (D)   70

19. Which story best fits the equation $9 + 6 = 15$?

   (A)   One student gives a teacher 9 pieces of candy, and another student gives the same teacher 6 pieces of candy. How many pieces of candy does the teacher have?

   (B)   A student gives her friend 9 boxes of candy. Each box has 6 pieces of candy in it. How many pieces of candy did the student give to her friend?

   (C)   A student has 15 pieces of candy and gives away 6 pieces. How many pieces are left?

   (D)   A student has 15 pieces of candy and puts the candy into boxes. If she puts 6 pieces of candy into each box, how many boxes are there?

20. A worksheet has 5 problems on it. If a teacher had to grade 14 worksheets, and she has already graded 6 of them, how many more problems does she have to grade?
   (A)   30
   (B)   40
   (C)   60
   (D)   70

21. While playing a trivia game, a player correctly answered 17 questions in the first half and 8 questions in the second half. If each question was worth 6 points, what was the player's final score?
   (A)   100
   (B)   125
   (C)   150
   (D)   175

22. A student was making baggies of cookies with 8 cookies in each bag. If the student had 77 chocolate chip cookies and 35 oatmeal cookies, how many baggies could the student make?
   (A)   13
   (B)   14
   (C)   15
   (D)   16

23. Which story best fits the equation $15 + 9 = 24$?

   (A)   A school has 15 classrooms, and I have 9 friends in each classroom. How many friends do I have?

   (B)   I have 15 friends. Over the summer, 9 of them transfer to different schools. How many friends do I have now?

   (C)   I have 15 friends, and I want to give each of them 9 pieces of candy. How many pieces of candy do I give away?

   (D)   I have 15 friends. On the first day of 4th grade, I make 9 new friends. How many friends do I have now?

24. A bookstore is offering a special deal: customers get $6 off when they purchase 7 books. If a customer bought 7 books and each book cost $6, how much would the customer's bill be?
   (A) $36
   (B) $42
   (C) $49
   (D) $56

Number Lines

Number lines were introduced in the Math Fundamentals section. Here, we will learn about some of the specific number line questions that may be tested on the Primary 4 ISEE.

Example #1
Use the number line to answer the question.

What three numbers are the vertical arrows pointing to on the number line?
(A)   4,   6,   22
(B)   5,   9,   23
(C)   6,   12,   22
(D)   6,   12,   24

Treat this as you would treat any number line question. You need to determine the increase that each tick mark represents. $21 - 3 = 18$. Then, divide by the number of equal spaces. $18 \div 6 = 3$. Therefore, each tick mark represents an increase of 3. $3 + 3 = 6$, so the tick mark to the right of 3 is equal to 6. You can eliminate (A) and (B). $21 + 3 = 24$, so the tick mark to the right of 21 is equal is 24. **(D) is the correct answer.**

Example #2
Use the number line below to answer the question.

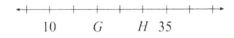

Point *H* is halfway between 10 and what number?
(A)   20
(B)   30
(C)   40
(D)   50

First, determine the value of each tick mark using the method discussed in Section III. The value of each tick mark is +5. That means the value of *H* is 30, because $10 + 5 + 5 + 5 + 5 = 30$. Now that you've labeled the number line, you can answer the question. 10 is four tick marks to the left of *H*, which means that the correct answer will be four tick marks to the *right* of *H*. $30 + 5 + 5 + 5 + 5 = 50$. *H* is halfway between 10 and 50, so **the correct answer is (D).** These questions are very advanced for 3rd grade. You should do easier questions first and complete these only if you have time remaining.

Practice Problems

1. Use the number line below to answer the question.

Which three numbers are the vertical arrows pointing to on the number line?
(A)   6, 12, 18
(B)   5, 8, 16
(C)   6, 10, 16
(D)   5, 12, 18

2. Use the number line below to answer the question.

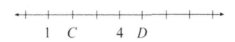

Point D is halfway between 1 and what number?
(A)   8
(B)   9
(C)   10
(D)   11

3. Use the number line below to answer the question.

Which three numbers are the vertical arrows pointing to on the number line?
(A)   0, 10, 25
(B)   3, 9, 28
(C)   4, 7, 9
(D)   0, 15, 25

4. Use the number line below to answer the question.

Which three numbers are the vertical arrows pointing to on the number line?
(A)   8, 10, 14
(B)   7, 8, 12
(C)   7, 8, 13
(D)   6.5, 7.0, 11.0

5. Use the number line below to answer the question.

Point F is halfway between 3 and what number?
(A)   33
(B)   34
(C)   35
(D)   36

6. Use the number line below to answer the question.

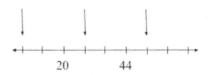

Which three numbers are the vertical arrows pointing to on the number line?
(A)   18, 21, 45
(B)   16, 22, 46
(C)   4, 28, 52
(D)   4, 26, 50

7. Use the number line below to answer the question.

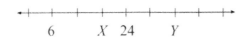

Point Y is halfway between 6 and what number?
(A)   30
(B)   36
(C)   60
(D)   66

8. Use the number line below to answer the question.

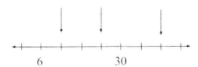

Which three numbers are the vertical arrows pointing to on the number line?
(A)   10, 18, 38
(B)   8, 12, 34
(C)   12, 24, 42
(D)   12, 18, 36

9. Use the number line below to answer the question.

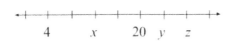

Point X is halfway between 8 and what number?
(A)   4
(B)   8
(C)   12
(D)   16

10. Use the number line below to answer the question.

Point Z is halfway between 10 and what number?
(A)   65
(B)   70
(C)   75
(D)   80

11. Use the number line below to answer the question.

Point Z is halfway between 10 and what number?
(A)   110
(B)   115
(C)   120
(D)   125

12. Use the number line below to answer the question.

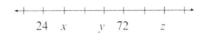

Point Y is halfway between 24 and what number?
(A)   72
(B)   84
(C)   96
(D)   108

Answer Key - Mathematics Question Types

Graphs	**Tables**	**Measurement**
1. B	1. C	1. C
2. C	2. D	2. B
3. B	3. A	3. D
4. B	4. C	4. A
5. C	5. C	5. D
6. D	6. D	6. D
7. B	7. B	7. D
8. C	8. B	8. B
9. A	9. B	9. A
10. D	10. C	10. C
11. C	11. D	11. B
12. D	12. A	12. A
13. B	13. C	13. D
14. B	14. B	14. A
15. D	15. B	15. B
	16. A	16. B
	17. C	17. B
	18. D	18. C
	19. B	19. B
	20. B	20. A
	21. D	21. B
	22. A	
	23. B	
	24. A	
	25. D	
	26. A	
	27. C	
	28. D	

Area and Perimeter

1. B
2. C
3. C
4. D
5. D
6. A
7. D
8. A
9. B
10. B
11. D
12. C
13. B
14. C
15. A
16. B
17. A
18. A
19. D
20. A
21. D
22. B
23. A
24. B
25. A
26. A
27. D
28. A
29. B
30. D
31. B
32. C

Patterns

1. B
2. C
3. A
4. B
5. A
6. C
7. B
8. D
9. C
10. B
11. A
12. A
13. D
14. D
15. B
16. D
17. C
18. C
19. B
20. A
21. B
22. C
23. C
24. D
25. D
26. A
27. D

Scales

1. C
2. B
3. B
4. C
5. D
6. A
7. C
8. C

Function Machines

1. D
2. C
3. A
4. D
5. C
6. A
7. C
8. D
9. A
10. A
11. B
12. C
13. C
14. D

Fractions

1. A
2. C
3. C
4. B
5. A
6. B
7. C
8. B
9. D
10. C
11. D
12. A
13. B
14. B
15. B
16. A
17. D
18. C
19. D
20. A
21. D
22. D
23. C
24. A
25. B

Estimating

1. B
2. D
3. C
4. A
5. A
6. C
7. B
8. C
9. D
10. C
11. B
12. B
13. C
14. D
15. A
16. D
17. C
18. A
19. D
20. B
21. D
22. C
23. A
24. B

Decimals

1. B
2. C
3. C
4. B
5. B
6. A
7. D
8. A
9. D
10. D
11. B
12. B
13. C
14. D
15. B
16. C
17. B
18. A
19. A
20. C
21. B
22. C
23. B
24. C
25. B
26. D
27. A

Net Shapes

1. B
2. B
3. A
4. D
5. A
6. D
7. B

Reflections and Lines of Symmetry

1. B
2. C
3. D
4. A
5. D
6. C
7. A
8. B
9. A
10. C
11. D
12. A
13. B
14. D

Coordinate Grids

1. B
2. C
3. D
4. C
5. B
6. A
7. D
8. D
9. D
10. A
11. D
12. B
13. D
14. C
15. B
16. A
17. C
18. D

Clue Tables

1. D
2. B
3. A
4. A
5. D
6. D
7. C
8. A

Charts

1. B
2. A
3. D
4. B
5. B
6. C
7. A
8. B
9. C
10. C

Symbols

1. B
2. B
3. C
4. A
5. D
6. A
7. B
8. C
9. C
10. D
11. A
12. A
13. A
14. A
15. B
16. A
17. D
18. B
19. C

Currency

1. C
2. A
3. D
4. C
5. B
6. A
7. A
8. D
9. C
10. B
11. B
12. A
13. D
14. C
15. D
16. B
17. B
18. C

Math Stories

1. C
2. A
3. D
4. B
5. D
6. C
7. C
8. B
9. A
10. B
11. A
12. D
13. C
14. B
15. B
16. D
17. A
18. D
19. A
20. B
21. C
22. B
23. D
24. A

Number Lines

1. A
2. B
3. D
4. B
5. A
6. C
7. D
8. C
9. D
10. B
11. A
12. C

Part V
Primary 4 ISEE
Mathematics Practice Tests

Practice Test #1

Practice Test #1 – 30 Minutes

1. A teacher created a graph to compare the sports that the students in his class play.

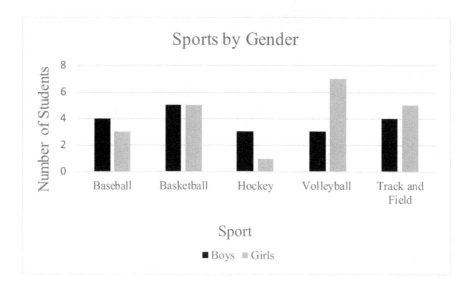

Which sport had the greatest difference between the number of boys and the number of girls who played that sport?
(A)   Baseball
(B)   Basketball
(C)   Hockey
(D)   Volleyball

2. Cody started looking for his missing cat at 4:35 P.M. If he found his cat at 7:50 P.M., how long did he spend looking?
(A)   2 hours and 5 minutes
(B)   2 hours and 15 minutes
(C)   3 hours and 5 minutes
(D)   3 hours and 15 minutes

3. Which fraction is equivalent to 0.6?

(A) $\frac{1}{6}$

(B) $\frac{1}{60}$

(C) $\frac{6}{10}$

(D) $\frac{6}{100}$

4. What is the sum of 4.7 + 2.4?
(A)   6.1
(B)   7.0
(C)   7.1
(D)   8.1

5. What is the name of a figure with 6 sides?
(A)   Pentagon
(B)   Heptagon
(C)   Hexagon
(D)   Octagon

Practice Test #1 – 30 Minutes

6. The table shows how many jumping jacks Rachel can do in a certain amount of time.

Number of Jumping Jacks	Minutes
25	1
50	2
75	3
100	4

At her current rate, how many jumping jacks can Rachel do in 8 minutes?
(A)   125
(B)   150
(C)   200
(D)   400

7. What units are most appropriate for measuring the weight of a pencil?
(A)   tons
(B)   grams
(C)   pounds
(D)   kilograms

8. Elie earns $22.24 per hour at her part-time job. Last week, she worked 8.78 hours. Which expression should she use to get the closest estimate of her pay?
(A) 20×9
(B) 25×8
(C) 22×8
(D) 22×9

9. Determine which choice best shows the commutative property of multiplication.
(A) $1 \times (3 \times 6) = (1 \times 3) \times 6$
(B) $1 \times (3 + 6) = (1 \times 3) + (1 \times 6)$
(C) $1 \times 3 \times 6 = 6 \times 3 \times 1$
(D) $1 \times 1 = 1$

10. Jeannine's dining room table can be lengthened by adding a 4-foot wide, 6-foot long section to the middle of it.

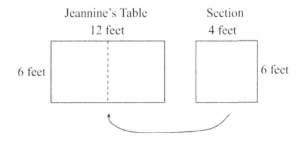

What will happen to the perimeter of Jeannine's table if she adds the 4-foot wide, 6-foot long section to the middle?
(A)   It will increase by 8 feet
(B)   It will increase by 10 feet
(C)   It will increase by 20 feet
(D)   It will increase by 24 feet

Practice Test #1 – 30 Minutes

11. Amaya recorded how much time she spent watching TV each day for 10 consecutive days.

TV TIME FOR AUGUST 12-21	
Aug 12	36.40 minutes
Aug 13	33.15 minutes
Aug 14	30.50 minutes
Aug 15	36.75 minutes
Aug 16	37.15 minutes
Aug 17	36.65 minutes
Aug 18	31.45 minutes
Aug 19	32.95 minutes
Aug 20	33.00 minutes
Aug 21	29.25 minutes

On which day did Amaya watch 1.50 minutes more of TV than she did the day before?
(A)   Aug 14
(B)   Aug 17
(C)   Aug 18
(D)   Aug 19

12. What is the value of the expression 1,000 − 435?
(A)   465
(B)   565
(C)   665
(D)   1,435

13. What is the standard form for three hundred ten thousand twelve?
(A)   301,012
(B)   301,120
(C)   310,012
(D)   310,120

14. The perimeter of the rectangle shown below is 36 cm. What is the length of side x?

12 cm

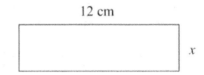

(A)   3 cm
(B)   6 cm
(C)   9 cm
(D)   12 cm

15. Jan has a box shaped like a cube. She cuts some of the edges to make the box flat. Which drawing shows the flattened box?

(A)

(B)

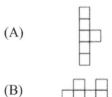

(C)

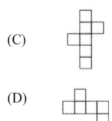

(D)

16. What is the value of the expression 402 + 319 + 12?
(A)   71
(B)   414
(C)   721
(D)   733

Practice Test #1 – 30 Minutes

17. The figure shows Jermaine and Monica's containers.

Jermaine   Monica

If each scale is balanced, which diagram shows that Monica's container weighs 2 pounds less than Jermaine's container? Let  = 2 pounds.

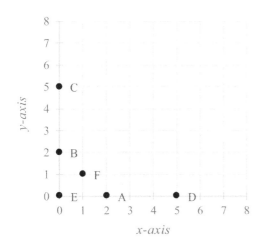

(A)

(B)

(C)

(D)

---

18. What are the coordinates of point *A* below?

(A)   (0,0)
(B)   (2,0)
(C)   (0,2)
(D)   (1,2)

19. A pattern is shown below.

What will the 8th figure in this pattern be?

(A)

(B)

(C)

(D)

Practice Test #1 – 30 Minutes

20. Determine what rule the function machine is using.

In	Out
4	1
12	3
20	5
28	7
40	10

(A) Plus 8
(B) Minus 3
(C) Times 4
(D) Divided by 4

21. What fraction of the figure below is unshaded?

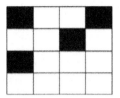

(A) $\frac{4}{16}$

(B) $\frac{1}{4}$

(C) $\frac{12}{4}$

(D) $\frac{6}{8}$

22. Markel brought some pieces of candy to school. He gave $\frac{1}{3}$ of the candy to his friend William, and $\frac{2}{3}$ of the candy to his teacher. If the teacher got 8 pieces of candy from Markel, how many pieces of candy does Markel have left?

(A) 0
(B) 1
(C) 2
(D) 3

23. Which decimal best represents the unshaded shapes below?

(A) 0.20
(B) 0.25
(C) 0.40
(D) 0.60

24. Jahmil solves a problem using the clue table.

Clue Table

In the equation $(\blacktriangle \times \blacktriangle) + (2 \times \bigstar) = 21$, what is the value of $\bigstar$?

(A) 5
(B) 6
(C) 7
(D) 8

Practice Test #1 – 30 Minutes

25. Shamell recorded the number of t-shirts each of his classmates bought on a shopping trip. Students 1 and 4 combined purchased 16 more shirts than student 3.

NUMBER OF T-SHIRTS PURCHASED

Student 1	👕👕👕
Student 2	👕👕👕👕👕
Student 3	👕
Student 4	👕👕
Student 5	👕👕👕👕

Based on the data, how many t-shirts are represented by the 👕 ?
- (A)   4
- (B)   8
- (C)   12
- (D)   16

26. The perimeter of the triangle below is 20 centimeters. The lengths of two of the sides are shown.

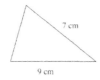

What is the length of the third side?
- (A)   4 cm
- (B)   5 cm
- (C)   6 cm
- (D)   7 cm

27. Which letter best shows $\frac{2}{3}$?

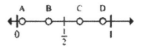

- (A)   A
- (B)   B
- (C)   C
- (D)   D

28. A total of 17 students were asked which one of three snacks – pizza, potato chips, or ice cream – they preferred. If 6 students said they preferred pizza, and 3 students said they preferred potato chips, how many students said they preferred ice cream?
- (A)   8
- (B)   11
- (C)   12
- (D)   14

MT

Practice Test #2

Practice Test #2 – 30 Minutes

1. The table shows the number of gifts Valentina wraps in a certain amount of time.

Gifts Wrapped	Minutes
3	6
4	8
5	10
6	12

At her current rate, how many minutes would it have taken Valentina to wrap 1 gift?
(A)   1
(B)   2
(C)   3
(D)   4

2. Mariana was drawing on scrap paper. She could fit 19 drawings on each page. If she has 121 pieces of paper, which expression shows approximately how many drawings she could make?
(A)   20 × 120
(B)   20 × 130
(C)   30 × 120
(D)   30 × 130

3. Kim is selling candy bars for her school.

Day	Bars Sold
Monday	3
Tuesday	6
Wednesday	9

If the pattern continues, how many candy bars will Kim sell on Friday?
(A)   3
(B)   12
(C)   15
(D)   18

4. The figure shows a drawing of Jose's bedroom

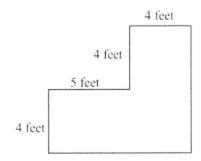

What is the perimeter of Jose's bedroom?
(A)   17 feet
(B)   23 feet
(C)   26 feet
(D)   34 feet

5. A student created the design below.

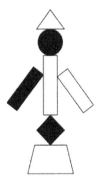

What fraction of the shapes in the student's design is shaded?

(A) $\frac{3}{4}$

(B) $\frac{4}{3}$

(C) $\frac{7}{3}$

(D) $\frac{3}{7}$

Practice Test #2 – 30 Minutes

6. Mr. Ower's dining room table can be lengthened by adding a 3-foot wide, 5-foot long section to the side of it.

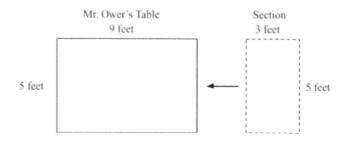

What will happen to the perimeter of Mr. Ower's table if he adds the 3-foot wide, 5-foot long section to the side?
(A)   It will increase by 6 feet
(B)   It will increase by 11 feet
(C)   It will increase by 15 feet
(D)   It will increase by 16 feet

7. What units are most appropriate for measuring the weight of a desktop computer?
(A)   kilograms
(B)   liters
(C)   ounces
(D)   tons

8. Jalisa's marble collection is shown.

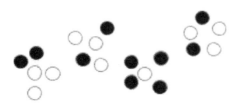

Which decimal represents the number of black marbles in Jalisa's collection?

(A)   0.25
(B)   0.50
(C)   0.75
(D)   1.00

9. A student knows that a door frame is about one meter across. Which object is about six meters tall?
(A)   a piano
(B)   a refrigerator
(C)   an adult person
(D)   a giraffe

10. The figure shows a drawing of Marty's bedroom

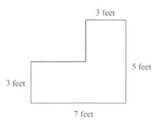

What is the area of Marty's bedroom?
(A)   18 square feet
(B)   24 square feet
(C)   27 square feet
(D)   35 square feet

Practice Test #2 – 30 Minutes

11. Determine which graph best represents the information in the table.

Name	Jess	Dorothy	Pierre	Aaron	Sid
States Lived In	3	1	4	7	5

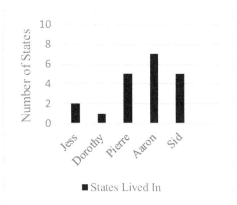

(A)

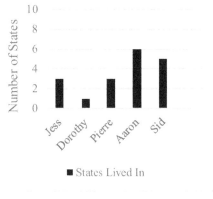

(C)

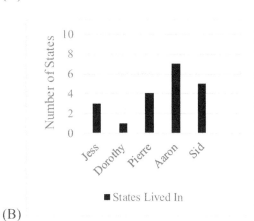

(B)

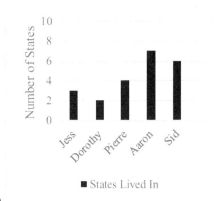

(D)

12. Which letter best shows $\frac{2}{8}$?

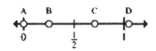

(A)   *A*
(B)   *B*
(C)   *C*
(D)   *D*

13. Which number has a digit in the thousands place that is twice the value of the digit in its tens place?

(A)   11,985
(B)   6,328
(C)   28,841
(D)   32,121

14. Luka has a box shaped like a cube. He cuts some of the edges to make the box flat. Which drawing shows the flattened box?

(A)

(B)

(C)

(D)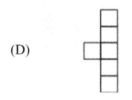

15. Determine what rule the function machine is using.

In	Out
19	14
27	22
32	27
33	28
36	31

(A)   Subtract 5
(B)   Subtract 8
(C)   Add 5
(D)   Add 8

16. Use the figure to answer the question.

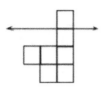

Which shows the figure after being flipped over the horizontal line?

(A)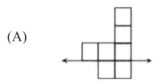

(B)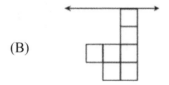

(C)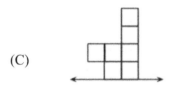

(D)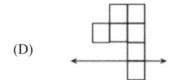

Practice Test #2 – 30 Minutes

17. The figure shows Nicola and Gustav's containers.

Nicola   Gustav

If each scale is balanced, which diagram shows that Gustav's container weighs 1 pound more than Nicola's container? Let ▢ = 1 pound.

(A)

(B)

(C)

(D)

---

18. Amina recorded how much time she spent practicing flute every day for 10 consecutive days.

PRACTICE TIMES FOR MAY 5-14	
May 5	17.50 minutes
May 6	28.45 minutes
May 7	19.50 minutes
May 8	15.00 minutes
May 9	29.95 minutes
May 10	24.30 minutes
May 11	25.75 minutes
May 12	29.98 minutes
May 13	21.20 minutes
May 14	20.68 minutes

On which day did Amina spend the greatest amount of time practicing flute?

(A)   May 6
(B)   May 9
(C)   May 10
(D)   May 12

19. What is the name of a figure with 9 sides?
(A)   Hexagon
(B)   Nonagon
(C)   Octagon
(D)   Heptagon

20. Which fraction is equivalent to 0.05?

(A) $\frac{5}{100}$

(B) $\frac{1}{50}$

(C) $\frac{5}{10}$

(D) $\frac{1}{5}$

21. What is the difference of 2.6 – 1.9?
(A)   0.07
(B)   0.70
(C)   1.70
(D)   4.50

Practice Test #2 – 30 Minutes

22. Yasmine draws a path on the coordinate grid. She begins at point (4,0) and moves 1 space right and 7 spaces up.

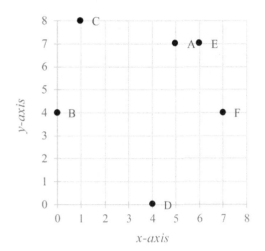

What is the point where Yasmine lands?
(A)   *A*
(B)   *B*
(C)   *C*
(D)   *D*

23. What is 1,456 rounded to the nearest thousand?
(A)   1,000
(B)   1,400
(C)   1,450
(D)   2,000

24. A student solves a problem using the clue table.

Clue Table

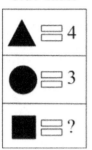

In the equation $(2 + \blacksquare) \times \blacktriangle = 28$, what is the value of $\blacksquare$?
(A)   3
(B)   4
(C)   5
(D)   6

25. Which expression is equal to $(5 \times 10) \times 9$?
(A) $(5 \times 10) + 9$
(B) $5 \times (10 \times 9)$
(C) $5 \times (10 + 9)$
(D) $5 + (10 \times 9)$

26. George brought some pieces of candy to school. He gave $\frac{3}{12}$ of the candy to his friend Jacob, and $\frac{5}{12}$ of the candy to his teacher. If George's teacher got 5 pieces of candy, how many pieces of candy did Jacob get?
(A)   1
(B)   2
(C)   3
(D)   4

Practice Test #2 – 30 Minutes

27. A teacher recorded the eye color of the students in his class. He counted 30 more students with blue and brown eyes combined than green and hazel eyes combined.

STUDENT EYE COLOR

Green	
Blue	
Brown	
Hazel	

Based on the data, how many students are represented by the  ?

(A)   6
(B)   7
(C)   8
(D)   9

28. The shaded part of the large rectangle represents a fraction.

Which point on the number line best represents the location of the fraction that is the shaded part of the rectangle?

(A)   P
(B)   Q
(C)   R
(D)   S

Part VI
*Answer Keys &
Interpreting Your Results*

MT

Answer Keys

Mathematics Answer Key – 28 Items
Practice Test #1

Item	Key	Your Answer	+ If Correct	*Type
1	D			D
2	D			N
3	C			N
4	C			N
5	C			G
6	C			A
7	B			M
8	D			N
9	C			A
10	A			M
11	D			D
12	B			N
13	C			N
14	B			M
15	D			G
16	D			N
17	D			A
18	B			G
19	B			A
20	D			A
21	D			N
22	A			N
23	D			N
24	B			A
25	A			D
26	A			M
27	C			N
28	A			D

*Key to Type of Item

N = Numbers and Operations
A = Algebraic Concepts
G = Geometry
M = Measurement
D = Data Analysis and Probability

Mathematics Answer Explanations – 28 Items
Practice Test #1

---

1. (D)   7 girls and 3 boys played volleyball. The difference is 4.

2. (D)   4:35 P.M. + 3 hours = 7:35 P.M. Then, add 15 minutes to get 7:50 P.M.

3. (C) $0.60 = \frac{60}{100}$. Divide the numerator and denominator by 10 to reduce the fraction to $\frac{6}{10}$

4. (C)   Stack the numbers, line up the decimals, and add as you normally would.

5. (C)   Pentagons have 5 sides, heptagons have 7 sides, hexagons have 6 sides, and octagons have 8 sides. You should memorize the names of shapes up to 10 sides.

6. (C)   Rachel does 25 jumping jacks each minute. She will do 125 jumping jacks in 5 minutes, 150 jumping jacks in 6 minutes, 175 jumping jacks in 7 minutes, and 200 jumping jacks in 8 minutes.

7. (B)   There are 2,000 pounds in 1 ton. There are 2.2 pounds in 1 kilogram. A pencil is too light to be weighed using tons, pounds, or kilograms.

8. (D)   22.24 rounds down to 22, and 8.78 rounds up to 9.

9. (C)   (A) shows the associative property of multiplication. (B) shows the distributive property of multiplication. (D) shows the identity property of multiplication.

10. (A)   Because the section is added to the middle of the table, only the top and bottom of the section will be included in the table's perimeter. 4 + 4 = 8.

11. (D)   On August 18, Amaya watched 31.45 minutes of TV. On August 19, she watched 32.95 minutes. 31.45 + 1.50 = 32.95.

12. (B)   1,000 – 400 = 600. 600 – 35 = 565.

13. (C)   Answers (A) and (B) would begin with "three hundred one thousand." Choice (D) is "three hundred ten thousand one hundred twenty."

14. (B)   The sum of the top and bottom of the rectangle equals 24 cm. 36 – 24 = 12. That means the two horizontal sides added together equal 12. 6 + 6 = 12, so (B) is correct.

Mathematics Answer Explanations – 28 Items
Practice Test #1

15. (D) (A) and (C) have 5 boxes in a row, so you can eliminate those. (B) cannot be folded to create a cube.

16. (D) Stack the numbers and add as you normally would.

17. (D) Use your own numbers. In choice (D), if Jermaine's container weighs 4 pounds, then Monica's container must weigh 2 pounds. On Monica's side, there is also a 2 pound block, which means there are 4 pounds on both sides of the scale, and the scale is balanced.

18. (B) In coordinate pairs, the number on the left represents how far left or right a point moves from the origin (0,0), and the number on the right represents how far up and down a point moves. Point A has moved 2 spaces to the right and 0 spaces up, so (B) is correct.

19. (B) In figure 6, the middle box will be shaded. In figure 7, the left box will be shaded. In figure 8, the right box will be shaded.

20. (D) In each row, the number on the left is divided by 4 to get the number on the right.

21. (D) 12 of the 16 squares are unshaded, so the fraction should be $\frac{12}{16}$. This is not an option, so you must find an equivalent fraction. (D) is the only equivalent fraction.

22. (A) You must first ask yourself, "$\frac{2}{3}$ of what equals 8?" $\frac{2}{3}$ of 12 equals 8, so Markel had 12 pieces of candy to start. $\frac{1}{3}$ of 12 is 4. Markel gave 4 pieces of candy to William and 8 pieces of candy to his teacher, leaving Markel with 0 pieces of candy.

23. (D) 3 of the 5 shapes are unshaded. $\frac{3 \times 20}{5 \times 20} = \frac{60}{100}$. Move the decimal in 60.00 two places to the left to get 0.60.

24. (B) First, plug in 3 for the triangles. $(3 \times 3) + (2 \times ★) = 21$. So, $9 + (2 \times ★) = 21$. Use the answer choices to work backwards. $9 + (2 \times 6) = 21$, so (B) is correct.

25. (A) The number of t-shirts purchased by students 1 and 4 is represented by 5 icons, while the number of t-shirts purchased by student 3 is represented by 1 icon. The difference is 4 icons. $4 \times 4 = 16$, so (A) is correct. You can also work backwards. Start with (A). If (A) is correct, students 1 and 4 purchased a total of 20 t-shirts, while student 3 purchased 4 t-shirts. $20 - 4 = 16$, which matches what the question tells you.

Mathematics Answer Explanations – 28 Items
Practice Test #1

26. (A) Perimeter measures the sum of all sides of a shape. $9 + 7 + 4 = 20$.

27. (C) If you break this number line into 3 equally sized pieces, there would be a tick-mark at Point B and at Point C. Point B represents $\frac{1}{3}$, and Point C represents $\frac{2}{3}$. Point A might be $\frac{1}{10}$, while Point D might be $\frac{9}{10}$.

28. (A) $17 - 6 - 3 = 8$.

Mathematics Answer Key – 28 Items
Practice Test #2

Item	Key	Your Answer	+ If Correct	*Type
1	B			A
2	A			N
3	C			A
4	D			M
5	D			N
6	A			M
7	A			M
8	B			D
9	D			M
10	C			M
11	B			D
12	B			N
13	C			N
14	B			G
15	A			A
16	D			G
17	D			A
18	D			D
19	B			G
20	A			N
21	B			N
22	A			G
23	A			N
24	C			A
25	B			N
26	C			N
27	A			D
28	C			N

*Key to Type of Item

N = **N**umbers and Operations
A = **A**lgebraic Concepts
G = **G**eometry
M = **M**easurement
D = **D**ata Analysis and Probability

Mathematics Answer Explanations – 28 Items
Practice Test #2

---

1. (B)   Valentina wraps 1 gift every 2 minutes. In 4 minutes she would have wrapped 2 gifts, and in 2 minutes she would have wrapped 1 gift.

2. (A)   19 rounds up to 20, and 121 rounds down to 120.

3. (C)   Kim sells 3 more candy bars each day. She will sell 12 candy bars on Thursday and 15 candy bars on Friday.

4. (D)   The horizontal sides of Jose's room are each 9 feet long. The vertical sides of his room are each 8 feet long. $9 + 9 + 8 + 8 = 34$.

5. (D)   Fractions are "part out of whole." There are 7 shapes total, and 3 of them are shaded in.

6. (A)   Perimeter measures the length of the outside of a shape. By adding the section to the side of the table, the top and bottom of the section will be included in the new perimeter. $3 + 3 = 6$.

7. (A)   Liters measure volume. Ounces are too small, and tons are too big. Kilograms are the most appropriate.

8. (B)   There are 10 shaded marbles out of 20 marbles total. First, make a fraction: $\frac{10}{20}$.
Then, multiply to make the bottom of the fraction equal 100. $\frac{10 \times 5}{20 \times 5} = \frac{50}{100}$. Move the decimal in 50.00 two spaces to the left to get 0.50.

9. (D)   6 meters is approximately 18 feet. The objects in answers (A), (B), and (C) are all much shorter than 18 feet.

10. (C)   The top, smaller portion of the room is 3 feet by 2 feet, so its area is 6 square feet. The bottom, larger portion of the room is 3 feet by 7 feet, so its area is 21 square feet. $21 + 6 = 27$.

11. (B)   This is the only graph that matches the information in the table.

12. (B) $\frac{2}{8} = \frac{1}{4}$. $\frac{1}{4}$ is less than $\frac{1}{2}$ but greater than 0. Point B is the only possible answer.

13. (C)   The tens place is the second number from the right. The thousands place is the fourth number from the right. 8 is twice the value of 4.

Mathematics Answer Explanations – 28 Items
Practice Test #2

14. (B)   (A) and (D) both have 5 boxes in a row, so you can eliminate those. (C) cannot be folded into a cube.

15. (A)   The difference between the left column and the corresponding right column is 5. Each number in the "out" column is 5 less than the number in the "in" column.

16. (D)   The given figure has 1 box above the horizontal line and 6 boxes below the horizontal line. Therefore, when the figure is flipped, there will be 1 box below the horizontal line and 6 boxes above the horizontal line. Only (D) works.

17. (D)   You can plug in your own numbers to find the correct answer. In (D), each box weighs 1 pound. If Gustav's container weighs 2 pounds, that means Nicola's container must weigh 1 pound. In this figure, there would be 3 pounds on the left side of the scale and 3 pounds on the right side of the scale, making it balanced.

18. (D)   29.98 is the greatest decimal of the 4 answer choices.

19. (B)   Hexagons have 6 sides, heptagons have 7 sides, octagons have 8 sides, and nonagons have 9 sides.

20. (A)   Move the decimal 2 places to the right to get 5, then put this number over 100. The answer is $\frac{5}{100}$

21. (B)   Stack the numbers, line up the decimals, and then subtract as you normally would.

22. (A)   Yasmine begins at Point D. If she moves 1 space to the right and 7 spaces up, she would land on Point A.

23. (A)   If the number is between 1,000 and 1,499 it rounds down to 1,000. If the number is 1,500 to 1,999 it rounds up to 2,000.

24. (C)   Plug in what you know. $(2 + \blacksquare) \times 4 = 28$. Then, use the answer choices to solve. Plugging in 5 gives you $(2 + 5) \times 4 = 7 \times 4 = 28$.

25. (B)   This question requires knowledge of the associative property of multiplication.

Mathematics Answer Explanations – 28 Items
Practice Test #2

26. (C)   If the teacher received 5 pieces of candy, and this represents $\frac{5}{12}$ of the total candy, that means there are 12 pieces of candy. Therefore, $\frac{3}{12}$ of the candy would equal 3 pieces.

27. (A)   You can work backwards. If each eye represents 6 students, then there are a total of 48 students with blue or brown eyes, and 18 students with green or hazel eyes. $48 - 18 = 30$. This matches what the question tells you.

28. (C) $\frac{7}{10}$ boxes are shaded. $\frac{7}{10}$ is greater than $\frac{1}{2}$, so the correct answer must be R or S. S is too close to 1, and most likely represents $\frac{9}{10}$

Interpreting Your Results

Interpreting Your Results

Once you've completed a practice test, check your answers using the answer key. Place a "+" next to each correct answer to determine your raw score (the total number of questions you answered correctly).

For the Lower, Middle, and Upper Level ISEE tests, the ERB releases a reported range & percentile rank chart to help students interpret their scores. This chart has not been released for the Primary ISEE tests, so we have recreated one using anonymized real scores from our own students. Please note that these scores do *not* reflect official guidelines from the ERB and are only approximate.

In theory, scores on the ISEE should form a classic bell curve, meaning most students score in the 4 – 6 stanine range, while only a handful of students receive a 1 or a 9. As you can see below, there are far more 7s, 8s, and 9s than you might expect. We believe this is because the Primary 4 ISEE is a difficult test, and very few students achieve a raw score of 20 or higher, leading to slightly skewed results.

ISEE Practice Tests Scaled Score Ranges (Min. = 400 and Max. = 499)				
Raw Score	Reported Range		Percentile Rank	Stanine
28	469	499	99	9
27	467	497	98	9
26	465	495	97	9
25	463	493	95	8
24	461	491	93	8
23	459	489	92	8
22	457	487	90	8
21	455	485	88	7
20	453	483	86	7
19	450	480	81	7
18	447	477	76	6
17	444	474	73	6
16	441	471	70	6
15	438	468	65	6
14	435	465	58	5
13	432	462	48	5
12	429	459	40	5
11	426	456	33	4
10	423	453	26	4
9	420	450	22	3
8	417	447	20	3
7	415	445	17	3
6	413	443	14	3
5	411	441	12	3
4	409	439	10	2
3	407	437	7	2
2	405	435	5	2
1	403	433	3	1
0	400	430	1	1

Made in the USA
Columbia, SC
24 October 2024

44983317R00111